The Wonderful World of

Nippon Porcelain

1891-1921

Kathy Wojciechowski

1469 Morstein Road, West Chester, Pennsylvania 19380

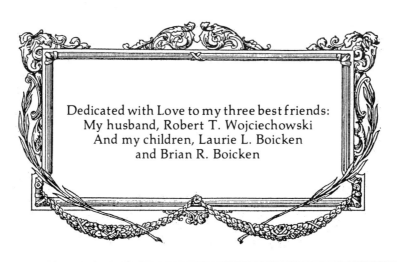

Dedicated with Love to my three best friends:
My husband, Robert T. Wojciechowski
And my children, Laurie L. Boicken
and Brian R. Boicken

Pedestal based calling card holder. 3¾" H. x 6¼" W. Maple leaf mark. Private collection.

Copyright © 1992 by Kathy Yates Wojciechowski.
Library of Congress Catalog Number: 91-67003.
Assisted by Cindy Yates Greenman

Printed in the United States of America.
ISBN: 0-88740-377-8

We are interested in hearing from authors with book ideas on related topics.

Published by Schiffer Publishing, Ltd.
1469 Morstein Road
West Chester, Pennsylvania 19380
Please write for a free catalog.
This book may be purchased from the publisher.
Please include $2.00 postage.
Try your bookstore first.

Contents

Enameled basket, 9" W. x 6¼" H. Collection of Lewis Longest, Jr., FP, CPP.

Original artist's sketchbook drawing, 1890. Nagoya, Japan.

Acknowledgments

The contents of this book give the reader the pleasure of viewing the top Nippon collections in the United States and Canada. The combination of these top collections offers readers the opportunity to view some of the finest Nippon objects know to collectors.

Many of my long time friends and collectors contributed so much to the completion of this book and to all of them I would like to express my deepest appreciation and gratitude, without their friendship, encouragement, cooperation and support The Wonderful World of Nippon would never have become a reality.

To my publishers Peter and Nancy Schiffer my sincere thanks for believing in this project and helping make this book a reality. Their faith and confidence frequently lifted my spirits and encouraged me to continue. Thank you both.

Thanks to my husband Butch, who has his own unique brand of encouragement and support as he took over many of my business and household functions so that I could continue with the research. He provided a never failing base of support and guidance that keep me motivated.

Thanks to Laurie Boicken, my daughter, who perpetually lives with a very busy mother, Laurie's love, encouragement and understanding wisdom far surpasses her seventeen years of age. I Love you LuLu.

Thanks to my son, Brian Boicken, whose command of the English language has made him my number one critic since he was ten years old.

Thanks to my sister, Cindy Greenman, for her quick green editing pen. It's been quite an experience for us to work together on this project—my grammar skills are terrible, her understanding of Nippon minimal and we frequently clashed heads on exactly how things were to be phrased. Through it all though, her never failing base of encouragement and enthusiasm enhances this book. As sisters we benefited by gaining a new understanding and appreciation for one other.

Thanks to my mother Norma Porter, her inner strength in the face of all odds, has been a living example of the path that I follow.

The number of hours Heinz and Darlene Damaske donated in assisting with the compilation of this book is a display of a giving friendship that I will always treasure. Heinz hand-drew the marks found on the Studio decorated items, and assisted Darlene with the doll research. Darlene hand-drew the doll marks and for many months made weekly trips (a four-hour drive) to my house where we put in long days categorizing and tagging over 1,100 photos. Many of these days were spent on our hands and knees on my office floor with photos laying everywhere, working on this book's organization. I sincerely thank both of you.

Thanks to my long time friend and business associate Harry Rinker, who was the first to suggest that I write this book, and over the years used his own personality and sharp tongue to prod me along. Thanks, Harry.

To my dear friend Rita Gills who lost her battle with cancer in May of 1991. Our long-standing friendship was based on the "we agree to disagree" policy and we had many, many long intense discussions which covered all aspects of Nippon and Nippon collecting. She was excited and so very supportive toward this project, she contributed valuable research information and many wonderful photos of her fine collection.

Thanks to Bob Gillis who took the time and energy to photograph his and Rita's collection at a most trying time in his life. I thank you for sharing your collection with us and for the moral support that you have always given me.

To my good friend Joan Van Patten who without her foresight in the production of her three Nippon books, my book would not have been possible. I first met Joan when I was a novice collector, her encouragement and guidance throughout the years has been important to me. She gladly shared useful and important research information, provided photos of her collection as-well-as lending her reproduction items for photographs seen in this book. Thank you Joan.

I also wish to thank my long-time friend Roger Zeefe, who has a spectacular Molded-in-relief collection, for his friendship, encouragement, contribution of photos, and unfailing support. Thanks, Roger.

Jan Dorland and Wilf Pegg were pioneers in the research of the color variations found in Molded-In-Relief items. These long-time friends contributed more valuable research information and many photographs of the color variations included in their large, impressive collection. Thank you both.

Other long-time friends are Bob, Flora, and Wesley Wilson whose extensive Wedgwood collection is a wonderful contribution to this book. They also contributed photos of non-Wedgwood items from their collection for use in this publication. Our children have grown up together and it has been a rewarding friendship for us all.

Jerry and Linda Cox spent many hours taking pictures and compiling descriptions of their exceptional Moriage collection for us all to enjoy. Their friendship and encouragement of this project have meant a great deal to me. Thank you so much.

Thanks to Harold and Audrey Eklund, whose diversified collection appears throughout several chapters. They have a wide range of pieces and I was anxious to include these beautiful photos in this book. I am grateful for their unconditional support.

Jess Berry and Gary Graves also contributed so much, they photographed numerous items from their collection spent a great deal of time compiling description lists, and even participated in the proof-reading of several chapters to verify information. Jess allowed me to re-print his article entitled "The ABC's of Nippon Collecting" which I believe will be enjoyed by collectors. Your contribution enhances this book and I thank you.

Philip and Jeanne Fernkes spent a great deal of time taking items from their collection to a professional photographer to ensure high quality photographs for use in this book. We started this project as acquaintances and ended as good friends, thank you so much.

Professional photographer and friend Polly Frye wrote "How To Photograph your Nippon Collection" for us to illustrate how to photograph your collection in a way that is non-threatening, even for the novice photo-grapher. Her advice serves as a valuable addition to my book. She also contributed photos of her collection and many photos of the marks. Thank You, Polly.

The Noritake Company's Vice President Osamu Tsutsui taped interviews that helped me reach higher understanding of the Noritake Company to share with you. Thank you also for your willing assistance with backstamp dating as well as the necessary background in understanding the history of the Morimura Brothers and the Noritake Company Ltd.

The others that I wish to thank for photos and/or research information include: George and Donna Avenzzano, Frank and Betty Bryson, Wayne and Barbara Bryant, Lee and Donna Call, Bartley and Catherine Casteel, Ralph and Cheryl DeWitt, Ted and Nita Ensign, Jan Eldridge, Dr. and Mrs. Jody Ginsberg, Pat Goan, Howard and Shirley Grubka, Olin and Grace Harkleroad, Rolfes and Virginia Hensley, Wayland, Brenda and Amy Horton, Stanley Jones, Cathy Keys, Catherine Lehor, Lewis and BJ Longest, William and Irma Lusson, Bill and Francile McLain, Norm and Fran Miller, George and Doris Myers, Wayne and Mary Myers (the dragon lady), Allan and Beverly Shaw, Cynthia Updike, and Andera L. Waysok.

Tapestry bottle neck vase 6½" H. Center medallion of swans on lake tapestry. Plaque 10" W.

Notes

The relentless search for additional verifiable Nippon information in regard to backstamp dating, numbers of certain items produced, and time span of production has been an almost impossible project for researchers. The majority of data about the Morimura Brothers and the very early Noritake Company was either lost through the years or destroyed in World War II. Bits and pieces of new information surface ever so slowly, and sometimes from these new tidbits we can develop a hypothesis of the probable relevance of this information.

New information reveals itself from many different sources. Some of these sources include out-of-date catalogues including several mail-order houses such as Montgomery Ward and Sears & Roebuck who actually advertised many Nippon items. The Larkin Soap Company is well known for its use of Nippon items as premiums for their soap-related products. Many Butler Brothers catalogs include pages of Nippon items offered for sale, categorically listed as Japanese China. Occasionally previously un-recorded pages from these catalogues do show up offering a glimmer of fresh information.

Of course there are hear-say stories circulating among collectors or dealers of Nippon, information that can not be substantiated. One such story is about a very unusual portrait "Jolly Monk" wine jug. It is unusual because a collector claims that in addition to the typical Nippon backstamp found on all monk wine jugs there are purportedly a number of these jugs which also bear a paper label reading "Compliments of the Salvation Army." If such an item indeed exists it would surely have marked a very special occasion for the Salvation Army, a religious and charitable organization established in 1865. Yet it apparently is an unmarked event in the organization's history. This filled wine jug, picturing a jolly monk drinking wine, was supposed to have been given away as a free gift. Repeated attempts to track down older Salvation Army records have produced frustratingly little.

Over the years collectors have had some heated arguments as to whether a vase required a lid. Many classical Nippon molds appear in the same size with and without lids. A vase which included a lid was then classified as an urn rather than a vase. How can we differentiate a vase which was intended to be without a lid and a vase of the same mold which was intended to have a lid? How can we know when we are looking at a complete Nippon item or at an urn which is missing a lid? The question is currently un-answerable, but according to some collectors there are catalogs or newspaper advertisements showing Nippon vases of the same size and shape offered with and with-out matching lids. If physical evidence of such publications indeed exists, it would certainly answer many questions.

The Sperry-Hutchison Company (which issued S&H Green Stamps) is believed to have carried Nippon items in their catalogues, yet very early S&H Green stamp catalogues are difficult to find making this information hard to substantiate.

On occasion a page or two from a salesman's sample book has turned up to further enlighten collectors. These unusual pages display exquisitely hand-colored drawings originating in Japan. Typically, these drawings have "Not for sale. Salesman's use" imprinted on the back. We believe that these books were used by American salesmen to show new selections and color variations to prospective buyers in the United States. There must be more of these sample pages in existence, yet we have been unable to locate them.

Undoubtedly there are other sources of information floating around just waiting for the right person to appreciate and record them. The author encourages readers to contact her with any additional information which comes to light. Whether it be advertisements, catalogues, newspaper clippings, or pictures of rare pieces. Verifiable corrections of any material covered in this book would be especially appreciated. Thank you in advance for contributing any information you may have.

A self-addressed, stamped envelope is appreciated and will facilitate a prompt reply. All letters will be answered. Kathy Wojciechowski P.O. Box 230 Peotone, Il. 60468

All non-attributed photos are from the Wojciechowski collection and were photographed by George Kwain Photography, Peotone, Il.

Original artist's sketchbook drawing, 1890. Nagoya, Japan.

Chapter One

History

In October of 1891, the McKinley Tariff Act was passed by the United States Congress, proclaiming that "All articles of foreign manufacture, be stamped, branded, or labeled and all packages containing such or their imported articles shall, respectively be marked, stamped, branded or labeled in legible English words so as to indicate the country of their origin; and unless so marked, stamped, branded or labeled in legible English words so as to indicate the country of their orgin; and unless so marked, stamped, branded or labeled they shall not be admitted to entry."

Nippon is the name for Japan, in Japanese. It derives from a Chinese term for "Land of the Rising Sun." Japanese exporters chose to comply with this law by marking their goods "Nippon."

The McKinley Tariff Act also set rules for the marking system, so that "all articles of foreign manufacture which are capable of being marked without injury shall be marked with country of origin in legible English words and marking shall be nearly indelible and permanent as the nature of the article will permit." Paper labels were acceptable and, in the case of small articles, *were* shipped together; only the inside and outside packages were marked with the country of origin.

In 1921, the U.S. government altered its position on the markings by determining that the use of the word "Nippon" was no longer in compliance with the law. "After examination into the history and derivation of the word "Nippon" and [consulting] lexicographers of recognized standing, the department is constrained to the conclusion the "Nippon" is a Japanese word, the English equivalent of which is "Japan," and the weight of authority does not support the earlier view that the word has become incorporated into the English language. All Japanese items must now be marked in English, "Japan." Thus, the Nippon era came to an end. Its short duration, between 1891 and 1921, is remembered by articles bearing the Nippon marks.

Sears, Roebuck catalog, 1908.

History of the Morimura Brothers and Noritake Co. Ltd.

As one begins to study the history of Nippon porcelain, one inevitably studies the history of Japan's export trade, for the two are undeniably interrelated. This fact inevitably enhances the study of these beautiful porcelain objects as they truly reflect a country's determination to change and to grow.

The historical account that follows is the publicly-released history supplied by the Morimura Bros., Inc. and Noritake Co., Limited. With their permission it is reprinted here. In addition, other pertinent information has been added to fill in a few missing pieces.

The Morimura Brothers company was born a full century ago when Morimura Gumi was founded, during the Meiji era—the era of "enlightenment and civilization." It was conceived in 1859 when young Ichizaemon Morimura, the sixth generation head of the Morimura family, recognized the opportunity to expand Japan's foreign trade. Morimura was from a Japanese merchant family and served as a member of the Japanese delegation to the United States in 1859.

After nearly 300 years of isolationism to world trade, the Tokugawa Shogunate was persuaded to open Japan's doors to the world in 1858. Two years later, in 1860 an envoy was dispatched to the United States to ratify the Treaty of Commerce and Navigation between the two countries.

Ichizaemon Morimura VI was assigned the task of providing the envoy with gifts and foreign monies. While carrying out this important assignment, he discovered that the monetary exchange rate was extremely unfavorable to Japan and feared that unilateral trade with resultant losses from such unfavorable exchange rates, if unremedied, would have a highly adverse effect on the future of Japan.

He consulted Professor Yukichi Fukuzawa, his friend and founder of Keio Gijyuka University, who advised, "There is no alternative but to increase exportation and thus get the money back to save the country."

Awakened to the importance of foreign trade, Ichizaemon, at the age of 22, resolved to dedicate his life to the realization of national prosperity on the basis of foreign trade.

In May of 1866, Japan's Shogunate took a bold step and permitted overseas travel in order to promote education and trade. Ichizaemon judged that the chance for expanding trade was drawing near and sent his younger brother, Yutaka, to study at the Keio Gijyuka University under the tutelage of Professor Fukuzawa, anticipating that he would become a future collaborator in potential business opportunities.

In an effort to meet his elder brother's expectations, Yutaka vigorously applied himself to his studies. He graduated with an outstanding academic record and later became an associate professor at his alma mater.

More than two years passed before the chance came in March of 1876, Yutaka boarded a 1200-ton commercial liner, named "Oceanie," at Yokohama Port bound for the United States. But before he departed, Yutaka and Ichizaemon founded "Morimura Gumi," a company that would later be known as a pioneer in the foreign trade industry.

Yutaka arrived in the United States and continued his studies for another six months before opening a retail shop on Front Street in New York in September, 1876. The shop was his first step in developing trade between Japan and the United States. The following year, Yutaka, with a new partner, started a new company called "Hinode Shokai" at Sixth Street, also in New York. In 1878, Yutaka terminated his partnership and independently founded "Morimura Brothers." Thus, Morimura Gumi was established in New York, in name and in fact.

In New York, Morimura had been continuously active in foreign trade. The company tried to appeal to the taste for art in the United States. In 1883, Yutaka shipped home to Japan a French-made coffee cup with a note stating that Japanese production of similar cups should begin at once. He considered these cups to be highly suitable to the U. S. market and envisioned that they would be of great help in developing future markets in the United States.

The Japanese ceramics industry had no experience in producing such a cup and, in fact did not even possess the necessary technology to accomplish the task even if they knew how. In collaboration with a potter in Seto, extensive studies were undertaken and technology developed to produce porcelain cups in Japan.

Morimura Gumi then committed all its resources to producing hard, white porcelain ware, with the objective of modernizing the chinaware industry.

Original artist's drawings, matted and framed, c. 1900 to 1920, samples for U.S. salesmen.

Imported Hand-Painted China Sets.

Sugar and Cream Set No. 109.

Price 90 cents when ordered with Products, Sold alone for $1.05. To mail 27 cts. postage required.

One Sugar-Bowl and one Cream-Pitcher. Decoration consists of combination border-and-spray design of berries and leaves in delicate tints of Blue, Green and Red, traced in Gold. Gold handles and edges. Height, 3 in. Diameter of Sugar-Bowl, 4 in.; Cream-Pitcher, 3½ in.

Chocolate Set No. 219.

Price $1.90 when ordered with Products, Sold alone for $2.10.

Consists of 6¼-in. Chocolate Pot and six Cups and Saucers. Decorated with pink flowers, buds, green leaves and white embossed work on chocolate-color background. Gilt edges and handles.

Cake Set No. 319.

Price $1.90 when ordered with Products, Sold alone for $2.10.

A Japanese, hand-painted Cake- or Bread-and-Butter Set. Consists of one 10-in. Cake-Plate and six 6-in. individual Plates. Has a border-design of pink roses and scroll-work with panels of pink roses and green leaves; center decoration of pink roses. Edges are gilt.

Nut Set No. 418.

Price $1.80 when ordered with Products, Sold alone for $2.

Set consists of one 6-in. Bowl and six 2⅝-in. individual Bowls. Decoration is white flowers and green leaves outlined in gold. Edges traced in gold.

Dresser Set No. 518.

Price $1.80 when ordered with Products, Sold alone for $2.

Set consists of Brush-and-Comb-Tray, 7⅝ x 10⅞ in.; Pin-Tray; Puff-Box; Hair-Receiver; Hat-Pin-Holder. Decoration is pink roses and green leaves with embossed work in gold.

Puff-Box and Hair-Receiver Set No. 610.

Price $1 when ordered with Products, Sold alone for $1.10. To mail, 30 cts. postage required.

Imported, hand-painted Puff-Box and Hair-Receiver. Has a conventional floral design of orange-colored blossoms and green leaves on a black background. Richly illuminated with gold. Diameter, 4 in.

Cups and Saucers Set No. 714.

Price $1.40 when ordered with Products, Sold alone for $1.60.

Six Teacups and six Saucers. Decoration consists of gold roses and panels of scroll-work, with pink roses and green leaves.

1912 catalog ad from Larkin Soap Company.

Imported Hand-Painted China.

Sugar and Cream Set No. 109.

Given with a $1.80 purchase of Products. To mail, 14 cts. postage required.

One Sugar-Bowl and one Cream-Pitcher. Decoration consists of combination border-and-spray design of berries and leaves in delicate tints of blue, green and red, traced in gold. Gold handles and edges. Height, 3 in. Diameter of Sugar-Bowl, 4 in.; Cream-Pitcher, 3½ in.

Chocolate Set No. 219.

Given with a $3.80 purchase of Products. To mail, 44 cts. postage required.

Consists of 9½-in. Chocolate Pot and six Cups and Saucers. Decorated with pink flowers, buds, green leaves and white embossed work on chocolate-color background. Gilt edges and handles.

Cake Set No. 619.

Given with a $3.80 purchase of Products. Cake or Bread-and-Butter Set. Consists of one 10-in. Cake-Plate and six 6-in. individual Plates. Has a border-design of pink roses and scroll-work with panels of pink roses and green leaves; center decoration of pink roses. Edges are gilt.

No. 619.

Cups and Saucers Set No. 714.

Given with a $2.80 purchase of Products. To mail, 50 cts. postage required.

Six Teacups and six Saucers. Matches Cake Set No. 619. Decoration consists of gold roses and panels of scroll-work, with pink roses and green leaves.

No. 714.

Nut Set No. 418.

Given with a $3.60 purchase of Products. To mail, 26 cts. postage required.

Set consists of one 6-in. Bowl and six 2⅝-in. individual Bowls. Decoration is white flowers and green leaves outlined in gold. Edges traced in gold.

Dresser Set No. 518.

Given with a $3.60 purchase of Products. To mail, 32 cts. postage required.

Set consists of Brush-and-Comb-Tray, 7⅝ x 10⅞ in.; Pin-Tray; Puff-Box; Hair-Receiver; Hat-Pin-Holder. Decoration is pink roses and green leaves with embossed work in gold.

Puff-Box and Hair-Receiver Set No. 610.

Given with a $2 purchase of Products. To mail, 14 cts. postage required.

Puff-Box and Hair-Receiver. Has a conventional floral design of orange-colored blossoms and green leaves on a black background. Richly illuminated with gold. Diameter, 4 in.

1913/14 catalog ad from Larkin Soap Company.

Item and stock number	*Larkin Catalogs.*	Price 1912	Price 1913/14
cream/sugar #109		$1.05	$1.80
chocolate set #219		$2.10	$3.80
cake set #319 & 619		$2.10	$3.80
nut set #418		$2.00	$3.60
dresser set #518		$2.00	$3.60
puff box, hair receiver #610		$1.10	$2.00
set 6 cups, saucers #714		$1.60	$2.80

The vision proved profitable as noted in *Japan at First Hand* by Joseph I.C. Clarke. In 1918 as the author describes in detail his visit to Japan, and his tour of the Morimuria Porcelain Factory.

A large part of their business is of smaller order of things for the cheaper grades of porcelain. One order amused me, namely, 11,400 cases of cups and saucers for 700 "ten cent stores" in the United States. Each case contains 300. So that these enterprising merchants of Uncle Sam account of 420,000 cups and saucers from Nagoya every year. What a mighty flood of gossip over the ten-cent tea cups this fact prefigures! They have a trade with England also in like ware and competed successfully with Germany.

On the first day of the new year in 1904, the chief executives of Morimura Gumi (Kotaro, Jitsuei Hirose, Kazuchika Okura and brother Magobei Okura, Yasukata Murai and Ichizaemon Morimura) founded Nippon Toki Gomei Kaisha, the forerunner of the Noritake Company Limited, to manufacture and export high quality chinaware mainly to the U.S. The United States has been Noritake's biggest customer since 1904.

The main office of Nippon Toki Gomei Kaisha was in a village called Noritake (now called Noritake Shin-machi, Nishi-ku, Nagoya City). According to Japanese tradition, this site was a rice field belonging to a powerful feudal clan called the Noritakes. Noritake China derives its name from this village where the company was originally located.

The technique to manufacture high-quality dinnerware was developed and mastered at this location in the 1910s and the Noritake company adopted streamlined mass-production systems over the next twenty years. The founders developed machinery to produce high quality wares in large volume.

In the course of the company's growth, subsidiary companies branched out to add to the prosperity of the Morimura Group.

For more than eighty years, the Noritake company produced pure white porcelain. Today, in addition to is superb china, Noritake also produces crystal glassware, flatware and a host of table accessories.

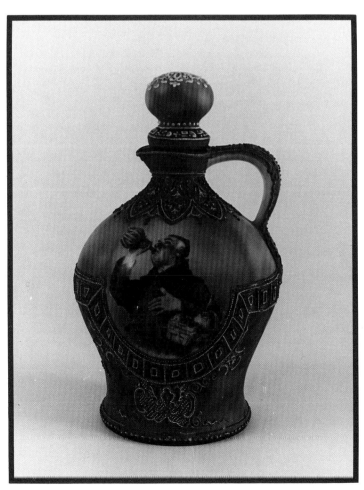

Monk wine jug 9½" H. Moriage trim. Collection of Frank and Betty Bryson.

In the Antiques world, and according to U.S. customs regulations, items must be a hundred years old to qualify as Antiques. By achieving the Antiques status, Nippon porcelains have become elevated to a higher plane of credibility and connoisseurs are understandably celebrating their transformation from "collectibles" to "Antiques."

Most items become collectible about twenty years after the end of their last production. For Nippon era items, this twenty-year anniversary fell in 1941, when the Japanese bombed Pearl Harbor. Anti-Japanese sentiment ran high during World War II. Many Americans removed the identifying marks from objects, so their friends wouldn't see that they had a Japanese item in their home. Even more Nippon items were discarded.

After the war, Japan's once-excellent industrial base was shattered; the main chinaware factory in Nagoya sustained grave damage. Equipment and raw material resources were limited. In the effort to rebuild their industry, Japanese companies manufactured inexpensive toys, carnival prizes, and give-a-way items that sold well. The backstamp "Made in Japan" became synonymous with low quality and high volume. After another forty years, collectors began to appreciate the earlier fine quality porcelain, great attention to detail and beauty of Nippon items.

The decoration of Nippon ware was, for the most part, dictated by the styles of the Western World. Porcelain objects were painted in Victorian, Art Nouveau, Edwardian and Art Deco styles. Tapestry techniques, achieved by pressing linen cloth on the soft, wet clay, and Wedgewood cameo techniques were occasionally used. Sometimes the colorful and bold Art Nouveau designs of Gouda ware from Holland were copied. Notable exceptions to the adoption of European motifs are primitive motifs from South American and ancient Middle Eastern style decorations.

The majority of Nippon items are hand painted with floral, natural and landscape designs. Heavily decorated and jeweled pieces were made in smaller quantity as were finely painted Victorian portraits. Animals and people were also popular subjects, particularly on items meant for men's use, such as ash trays, steins, mugs and tobacco humidors. Frequently the animals and people designs were molded-in-relief, giving the objects a three-dimensional appearance. Moriage techniques and Coralene decoration were used as embellishments on Nippon porcelain.

Appreciation for the beauty of the hand-painting and high quality of the porcelain in Nippon wares has grown more widespread over the last fifteen years. As demand has grown greater than the supply, prices have climbed dramatically.

Collecting is somewhat an extension of yourself. As a collector, you should choose what is most appealing to you and your lifestyle. Educate yourself before beginning to collect. Read everything you can find and be familiar with the three counterfeit Nippon marks; once you have seen both the authentic and the bogus marks, it will be VERY easy to determine the difference.

Damaged and repaired items should be purchased only at reduced prices. A damaged item today will be a damaged item ten years from now while an undamaged, high quality piece will probably escalate in value.

Buy the best you can afford. If you have $400 to spend, you can buy four mediocre pieces or one, fine-quality $400 piece. Ten years from now, the $100 pieces will still be mediocre, and the $400 piece will still be fine quality but most likely will have increased farther in value.

What is rare?/Market report

Funk and Wagnalls dictionary defines the word "rare" as "the infrequent in occurrence, distribution, etc.; highly esteemed because of the infrequency or uncommonness."

Based on this definition then, what objects would be considered Nippon rarities?

Many people think that Nippon rarities are necessarily expensive rarities, and in many instances this is simply not true. Yet there are many rare Nippon objects that are relatively inexpensive.

Over the years, items which Nippon collectors once thought to be rarities have surfaced in large enough quantities to indicate that they are in fact quite plentiful. Conversely, other items that were plentiful years ago and taken for granted have since become rare and highly collectible.

Twenty years ago, when molded-in-relief items were beginning to surface, collectors became enamored with plaques, humidors, vases, etc. which were previously believed to be rare.

As more and more information about these "rarities" was released to the general public, and as prices reached all time highs, Nippon molded-in-relief items started turning up quite regularly. People who had these items for many years, but were unaware of their value, now brought them out into the open market.

Chocolate pot, 12½" H. Unmarked. Collection of Wayland and Brenda Horton.

Several of these items once thought to be rare, have now reached the common status. Such as the lion and lioness, moose, stag, buffalo, Indian on horseback, and squirrel. Conversely, other molded-in-relief items that were rare twenty years ago have escalated to a "Super Rare" status. These items are highly collectible, and no amount of advertising telling of increased values has flushed these items from grandma's attic. Collectors who have these items in their collections are aware of the increased difficulty in obtaining them and have no intention of selling what items they already have. All indications lead us to believe these items will continue to remain very rare.

Very large "palace urns," 24" high and larger, have become highly prized by collectors; only one or two of these large urns appear on the market per year. These magnificent urns were assumed to have been made in much smaller quantities for very special people or occasions. With less of these items being produced their rarity is ensured.

Any Nippon item made with a lid, such as bolted covered urns, covered urns, or humidors have recently achieved a new level of respect and collectability. Between 1891 and 1921, when Nippon items were mass-produced, sold inexpensively and treated accordingly, many of these items were used on a daily basis with little thought to future value or collectability, when lids to items were broken and discarded. Few items can be found today with the original lids intact. And when such treasures are found they are commanding very high prices.

The very early Victorian ornate portrait items which were lavishly decorated with heavy gold overlay designs, gold beading and multi-colored jewels presumably were not mass-produced in the quantities that other more readily found Nippon items were as there scarcity indicates. Another factor to consider when analyzing the scarcity of Portrait items is that as the Japanese increased production of their wares and modernized decoration techniques, less attention and time was allowed for decorating each item. It is commonly believed that heavily decorated, ornate portraits were phased out in favor of items which could be decorated quickly.

Other items which were plentiful twenty years ago have become rare. For instance, small toiletry items such as talcum shakers, ladies spittoons, toothbrush holders, shaving mugs, mustache cups and saucers, ring trees, perfume bottles and hat pin holders were plentiful, inexpensive and were damaged in every day use and disposed of with little thought of their future collectability. Today, these items are considered scarce.

Tankard, 14" H. Oriental China mark. Howard and Shirley Grubka collection.

1915 Larkin Soap Company catalog for Groceries and Home Supplies #27 are apparently the first examples of Noritake Azalea pattern distributed by Larkin. Azalea did not appear in the regular Larkin Catalog until 1923/24.

Bowl, 4½" W. Collection of Wayne and Barbara Bryant.

Dresser set. Tray, 12¼" W. x 10" H. Candlesticks, 5½" H. Open hat pin holder, 5¼" H. Hair receiver and powder box, two covered jars, and pin tray. Kinjo China, two fish Nippon mark. Harold and Audrey Eklund collection.

Marked Nippon verses Unmarked Nippon

The question of authentic unmarked Nippon versus authentic marked Nippon pieces still enters the minds of many collectors and dealers alike. Should unmarked Nippon pieces be added to one's collection? If a decision is made to purchase an unmarked item, should there be a price differential between unmarked and marked items? Should unmarked pieces be dismissed entirely? These questions pose a dilemma for many collectors. There are many Nippon purists who believe that if an item does not bear the Nippon backstamp it simply is not Nippon.

Entering into a new area of collecting does require a determination to gain knowledge, a financial commitment and the desire to tread lightly until collecting confidence has been developed. Novices tend to buy only marked items.

New collectors often ask whether there are authentic unmarked Nippon items available on the market today. The United States is protected by the McKinley Tariff Act of 1891 which states that "All items of foreign manufacture which are capable of being marked without injury shall be marked with the country of origin in legible English words and marking shall be as nearly indelible and permanent as the nature of the article will permit."

There were many reasons that genuine Nippon pieces were indeed allowed into the United States unmarked. Some items were too fragile or too small to be marked properly and some items belonged to a set in which only one piece was required to be marked. Further, on groups of items packed within the same shipping crate, based on

this act, only one piece was required to be individually marked. Some items consist of two or more pieces (such as a condensed milk container which has a jar, lid and underplate) only one of which would bear a Nippon backstamp. Items intended for exportation to the United Kingdom did not require a Nippon backstamp during this time period. Some genuine Nippon items were shipped to the United States bearing no Nippon backstamp, but removable paper labels.

Certainly there are objects which qualify as true Nippon that did come into the United States unmarked. One can find similar items manufactured in Austria, Germany and other European countries. The buyer must beware.

How does a collector know how to identify for himself whether an item is indeed unmarked Nippon or a piece of unmarked porcelain manufactured elsewhere? This is not an easy task since the Japanese were talented in duplicating porcelain and are believed to have copied many Austrian, German, and French mold designs and decoration designs.

For the collector new to the world of "Nippon" a degree of caution is advised until a "feel" for authentic Nippon is developed. Only the thoughtful handling and viewing of many pieces over a length of time qualify a person to make an accurate judgment about the period and origin of an unmarked item thought to be Nippon. It's not difficult, but it does require exposure to a number of these items and some degree of background study.

Imported Hand-Painted China

Celery Set

No. 1513 GIVEN with a purchase of Products or for $3.50 in Coupons.

This handsomely decorated Celery Set will add greatly to the attractiveness of your table appointments. Set consists of one Celery Tray, 12⅜ x 6¼ in., and six individual Salt-Trays. Decorated in a conventional border design of green leaves and flowers, richly illuminated in raised gold. Edges outlined with gold. Shipping weight 4 lbs.

Bon Bon Dish

No. K1110 GIVEN with a $2.50 purchase of Products or for $2.50 in Coupons. Diameter, 7 in. Inside decoration consists of a landscape with lilies in natural colors in the foreground. Has fancy gold border outside. Burnished gold edges and handles. Shipping weight 3 lbs.

Dresser Set

No. 717A GIVEN with a $4 purchase of Products or for $4 in Coupons.

This set of delicately-ornamented, hand-painted China toilet-articles will delight the heart of any woman. Matches Manicure Set 192010 in opposite column. Set consists of Brush-and-Comb-Tray, 7½ x 10⅜ in.; Pin-Tray; Puff-Box; Hair-Receiver; Hat-Pin-Holder. Decoration is pink roses and green leaves with embossed work in gold. Shipping weight 6 lbs.

Condiment Set

No. 709 GIVEN with a $2.50 purchase of Products or for $2.50 in Coupons.

Set consists of Tray, 7 x 5 in., Mustard-Jar with Spoon, Tooth-Pick-Holder and Salt- and Pepper-Shakers. Decoration is a conventional design in burnished gold. Shipping weight 2 lbs.

Jam Jar Set

No. 49010 GIVEN with a $2.50 purchase of Products or for $2.50 in Coupons.

An attractive container for jam, marmalade or condensed milk. Set consists of Jar, 3¾ in. high, Plate 6½ in. in diameter, and Ladle. Decorated with pink, white and red roses, blended with shaded leaves. Edges are outlined in gold. Shipping weight 3 lbs.

Manicure Set

No. 192010 GIVEN with a $2.50 purchase of Products or for $2.50 in Coupons.

Set consists of 7¾-in. Tray, oblong Powder-Box and three different size jars that can be used for cold cream, powdered pumice, cuticle-ice, etc.

Decoration is pink roses and green leaves with embossed work in gold. Matches Dresser Set 717A. Shipping weight 2 lbs.

China Tea-Plate Set

Price, $2.50

Dainty, hand-painted imported China Tea-Plates, prettily decorated with pink-and-white azaleas and green leaves. Edges of Plates outlined in gold. Set consists of six Plates, 7½ in. in diameter. A very pretty Set especially desirable for use on exceptional occasions. A charming Set for the china-cabinet.
Shipping weight 4 lbs. 9 oz.

China Whipped-Cream Set

Price, 90c

A charming Whipped-Cream or Mayonnaise Set of hand-painted imported China, daintily decorated with pink-and-white azaleas and green leaves, to match China Tea-Plate Set.

Edges are outlined in gold. Set consists of Plate, Bowl and Ladle. Bowl 4½ in. in diameter. Plate, 5½ in. in diameter. Appropriate for serving any sauce or dressing. Shipping weight 1 lb. 9 oz.

China Salt and Pepper Shakers

Per pair, 50c

Genuine China Shakers, each made in one piece in very attractive fluted design. Not easily upset.

Old-ivory color prettily decorated with large pink rose, green leaves and gold band around top. Filled through bottom. Dainty and ornamental. Each shaker 2½ in. high.
Shipping weight 6 oz.

China Teacup and Saucer Set

Price, $2.50

A beautiful set of hand-painted imported China Teacups and Saucers. Azalea decoration; gold outlined edges and gold line on handles. Match China Tea-Plate Set. Light and dainty.

Just the thing for afternoon tea or a special occasion. Set consists of six Teacups and six saucers. Shipping weight 6 lbs. 1 oz.

China Butter-Tub and -Drainer

Price, 85c

A pretty Butter-Tub of translucent vitrified china decorated with a delicate apple-blossom design. Edges and handles are decorated with coin gold lines. Drainer is separate piece decorated with coin-gold line. Diameter of Tub at top, 5 in. Height, 2 in.
Shipping weight 2 lbs. 7 oz.

Earthenware Set

or

White-Lined Baking Set

Price, $3

A practical Baking Set of glazed brown earthenware. White-lined and very durable. Consists of the following pieces:

One 1-qt. Casserole
One 1½-qt. Casserole
One 1⅜-qt. Pudding-Dish
One 2½-qt. Pudding-Dish
One 9-in. Pie-Plate

This ware is recommended and used by domestic science experts. It is much superior to metal utensils and is ideal for puddings, pies, macaroni, noodles, custards, short-cakes, potato dishes, meat pies and for dishes made from left-over meats and vegetables.
Shipping weight 24 lbs.

1917-1918-Larkin Soap Catalog. Prices for the Imported China were increased over the previous catalog.

Pair of footed vases 7¼" H. M-in-wreath mark. Collection of Phil and Jeanne Fernkes.

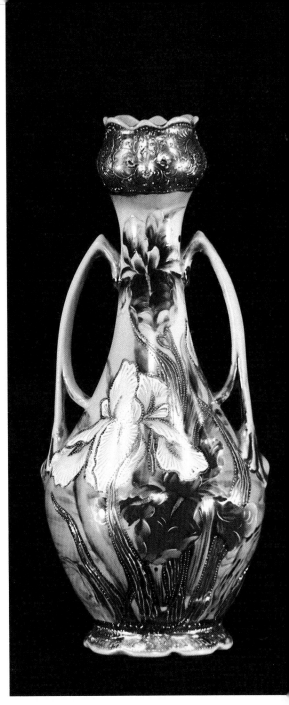

11¼" H. M-in-wreath mark. Collection of Phil and Jeanne Fernkes.

The major factor in determining the origin of an unmarked item is the feel of the overall object and the quality and weight of the porcelain itself, which will tell you if the item is Nippon or a heavier weight lower-quality porcelain European-made object. Varied as it is, Nippon porcelain has a unique personality of its own, even though designs were copied from French, German, and English (Wedgwood) factories during the same 1891-1921 period. Nippon has a look and feel that is truly distinctive. The expressive art work, characteristic style, gold beading, relief work, scenic matte finish, cobalt, gold and rose motif characterizes true Nippon items.

Nippon's distinctive personality becomes clear to a collector slowly, he must handle as many marked Nippon items as possible until he instinctively becomes comfortable with understanding the characteristic feeling of genuine Nippon.

In order to learn this "feel" for yourself first rub your hand lightly over the surface, next gently weigh the object back and forth from one hand to the other, close your eyes while doing this, concentrate only on the object in your hand. Your hands can tell you if the weight and balance is Nippon correct.

After you have handled many marked Nippon items and begin to understand the "feel," start handling unmarked items that you suspect to be Nippon. Remember that just because someone has written unmarked Nippon on a price tag it does not necessarily make it an authentic piece of unmarked Nippon. The collector himself must be able to "feel" the Nippon qualities and make the judgement himself.

The most prevalent examples of authentic items available both with and without a Nippon backstamp are "gaudy" items with all over decoration and no white showing.

Many Nippon collectors will not purchase an unmarked piece of Nippon, yet conversely many collectors are partial to unmarked Nippon items. Beauty and artistic design are and will continue to be the guideline in determining the desirability in porcelain art collecting, marked or not. Generally speaking collectors will pay less for an unmarked item than they would pay for a identical item bearing an authentic Nippon backstamp.

When purchasing a marked or unmarked item the choice lies completely with each collector.

Collectors' opinions regarding unmarked Nippon items are mixed and varied in relation to geographical location. Some states show a definite preference to "gaudy" unmarked items with little or no interest in the scenic items, while other states prefer the scenic items with little or no interest in the gaudy unmarked florals. In the southern states of America from Kentucky to Georgia, and from the Mississippi River east to the Carolinas, the most desirable Nippon items are gaudy floral bowls, chocolate sets, tea sets, pitchers, vases, tankards, plates and plaques which are often unmarked. They are noted for their vivid colors and use of heavy gold overlay designs with ornate gold trimmings. In the same geographical area, one rarely finds bisque scenic items. On the other hand, in the east and west coasts, collectors prefer the hand-painted scenic items.

Prices of certain items reflect these geographical preferences and therefore the less favored items can be purchased more reasonably in the states showing favoritism to the other styles.

Misunderstandings about the Green, Blue, Magenta Marks

Many Nippon backstamps, (including the "M-in-wreath" mark, the "Maple leaf" mark, "Cherry blossom" mark, "Rising Sun," and others) can be found in three color variations: green, blue and magenta.

There has been much discussion over the years regarding the actual meaning attached to these three color variations found on Nippon backstamps.

The Noritake Company has indicated that the three colors correspond to a grading system: green for first grade, blue for second grade, and magenta for third grade. But the company had been unable to explain what "first, second, and third grade" describes or refers to. Does the grading system refer to the quality of the art work, the quality of the porcelain, or perhaps a combination of both?

The blue maple leaf mark was applied to differentiate body blanks which were produced by Mourimura's subcontract factories rather than those of their own factory. Other factories were commissioned to produce blanks at a time when Morimura or Noritake did not

Covered urn 11" H. Gold overlay butterflies, on top of spider web. Unmarked. Private collection.

have a factory. The Blue Maple leaf mark appears only on pieces produced at the subcontract factories.

Most of the remaining historical records regarding the Morimura and Noritake Company during the Nippon era were destroyed during World War II. Therefore, no definitive information is available today.

Nippon collectors have believed one of three possible explanations in regards to the meaning of these three different colors: 1. the quality of art work, 2. the quality of the porcelain used in producing each item, and 3. a combination of both of the above.

Noritake Company's notion of the grading system is based on the symmetrical formation of the blank body and on the degree of imperfections in the porcelain. So #2 above is partly factual, while the grading system does refer to the quality of porcelain, it further is based upon the symmetrical formation of the blank body. And has no reference to the quality of the art work.

Each blank was inspected very carefully before a backstamp was added. To an item that was perfectly symmetrical with no imperfections, a green backstamp was given. For an asymmetrical body with slight imperfections, a blue backstamp was given. The magenta mark was given to items showing both imperfections in the body and quality of porcelain.

Today, one finds the magenta backstamp primarily on utilitarian table items such as salt and pepper shakers, cream pitchers, sugar bowls, celery sets and children's dishes.

The Noritake Company also has indicated that the three colors identified the original producing factory and markets in which they were sold, in addition to the differences in quality.

Some people wonder whether an item with a certain color mark is worth more money than the same item with a different color mark. The color of the mark should have no bearing on a price. Everything about the item should be taken into consideration: art work, quality of porcelain and appeal.

L. "The Angelus" (1857-1859) R. "The Gleaners" (1814-1875) both vases are based on oil paintings on canvas by the famous french painter Jean Francoins Millett. He is well known for his French genre and landscape paintings of the Darbizon school. Most renown for "The Augelus" and "The Man with a hoe". Rare. 12" H. M-in-wreath mark. Collection of Rolfes and Virginia Hensley.

Chapter Two

Quality of Art Work

The quality of the art work is an extremely important consideration. In the 1890s, the Morimura Brothers main objective was to organize groups of people from independent Japanese decorating houses, and provide these decorators with blanks to decorate.

The Morimura Brothers purchased blanks from other potters in Japan and imported an even larger amount of blanks from Limoges, France. All of these blanks were backstamped with the Morimura Brothers mark and sent to various china painters in Japan to be decorated.

Items of the same blanks went to different decorating houses. In an effort to control the aesthetics of the finished products and to give individual artists guidelines toward the finished work, the Morimura Brothers included a sketch indicating color placement or, in some instances, an outline of the scene lightly traced on the item. This attempt for continuity was only partly successful since each artist lent his interpretation on every piece he painted.

Most of the china painting houses were family-owned operations where several people participated. Here, items were painted by different artists, each with a specific area to paint. For example, one would paint the background, another the trees, and yet another the main focal object, etc. For this reason, one seldom finds Nippon items signed by an artist. The practice of several artists working on one item was more common than a single artist working entirely on his own.

Each artist had his own interpretation of the design, and possessed varying degrees of artistic ability. Therefore, the quality of art work, shading of colors and definition of design seen in the finished products vary considerably.

Better art work produced a more desirable object, and commanded a higher price.

ABC's Of Nippon Collecting By Jess Berry

Always take care when considering a selection. Be particular of what you add to your collection. Check carefully for damage or the hidden repair. Desirable items should be chosen with care. Excitement and eagerness are part of the game. Fascination in abundance when Nippon is the name. Gold frequently was used with beading in a row. Handles and finials with gold often glow. If you're one of the lucky ones, you may even find Jasperware pieces that are one of a kind. Kiss your good luck charm and always remember Luck such as this comes only on the 31st of September! Moriage trimmed items have to admire Nippon with this treatment is good to acquire. Overlays of gold add special attraction Purchases of such pieces gives great satisfaction. Quality Nippon represents things well worth owning Reproduction pieces have us groaning and moaning. Study and absorb the Nippon information you find Take the necessary effort to keep it in mind. Using all the knowledge you manage to acquire Very carefully you can build a collection to admire. Wonderful Nippon goodies are just waiting for you Xtra searching may turn up a dozen or two. You can spend whole days Nipponing with excitement and pleasure Zest and zip to your life you will add in full measure.

Care

Collectors enjoy watching an item coated with years of dirt and grime come alive by careful washing. A few simple cleaning guidelines are offered: To wash an item, first line the sink bottom with foam rubber, or a folded bath towel to prevent accidental breakage when the item taps the bottom of the sink. Avoid using very hot or very cold water as extreme external temperature may cause damage. Never put Nippon items into a dishwasher. Use only warm water and a mild soap.

One method is to let the item soak for ten or fifteen minutes. Then, using a soft sponge, carefully wash the entire surface and rinse the soap off. The object can air-dry or be wiped with a soft towel.

Another washing method (my favorite) is to stand the item on a secure flat place and spray the object with a household cleaning product such as "Fantastic," ("409" is a stronger solution and should be used cautiously). Let the spray drip down the item, and spray again. This can be done several times. You will know when to stop when the liquid that runs off is no longer dirt-filled. Next, submerge the item into the sink, use a soft sponge to wipe it clean, and then rinse. On items with gold handles or trim a soft buffing with a soft towel or cotton ball highlights the gold.

Occasionally, dark marks are not removed by the methods mentioned and a little extra attention is required. On these hard to clean areas, a mild abrasive such as "softscrub" or "409" and gentle buffing should remove them. If you have tried these methods and the mark is still not removed, stop-do-not try anything harsher. The dark mark may be under the glaze and not removable without damaging the finish.

Every day preservation includes placing objects out of the reach of small children, large dogs, inquisitive cats, and away from heavy traffic areas such as foyers and door ways.

China cabinets protect items from dust and frequent handling.

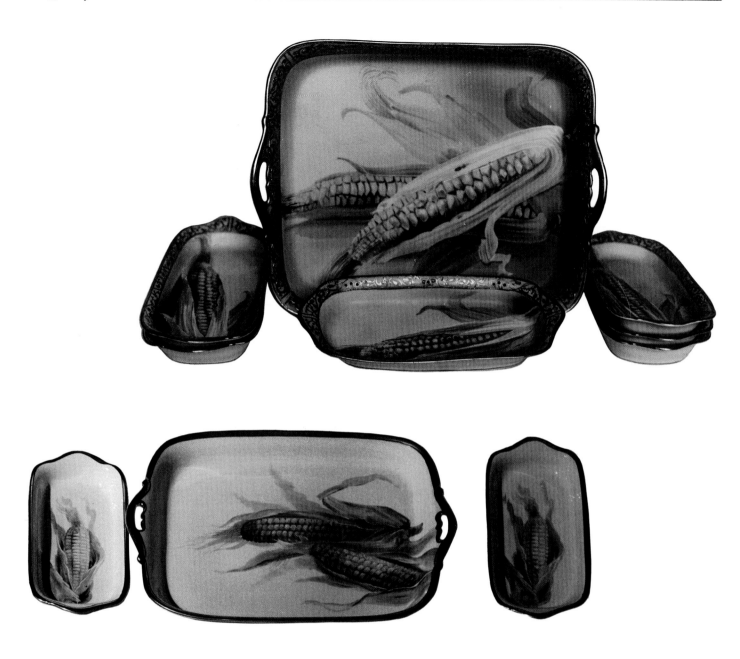

These two corn sets show a perfect example of the wide range in the quality of art work. Both large platters are 12½" W., both items are marked with the "M-in-wreath" mark, yet the attention given to the art work in the kernels of corn, the background shading, and the intricate design of gold over-lay, with multi-colored jewels added to the border, make this set more desirable than the plain version.

1) Plaque 10" W. (2) Bowl scalloped edge 10½" W. (3) Cake plate, pierced handles 10½" W. The difference in the art work on these three items is not as pronounced as that of the difference shown on the corn sets, but if you study closely the art work shown on these three objects you will detect subtle differences in the art work on each. It is these slight differences that truly affect the market value of any given object.

Photo 1

Photo 2

These three plaques are perfect examples of the same mold decorated with different degrees of art work, and also show drastic differences in color variations.

Photo 1 shows the basic mold decorated with a brown wash. This Indian appears to be standing in ankle deep water without a ripple in the water or a body shadow cast by the sun. The goose hanging over his back has no noticeable definition.

Photo 2 shows the same basic mold with the addition of many colors, and well-defined features. This artist added ripples in the water, a shadow cast by the sun and some very faint background designs. The goose is rendered in shades of blue-gray with the only contrast shown in his white beak.

Photo 3 shows the creative talents of a fine artist. This Indian is standing in tall grasses on the bank of the water rather than in the water itself. The goose is well-defined with more natural coloring. A large tree has been added to the background with its branches extending across the top of the plaque. And there is a definite tree area in the distance.

If you as a serious collector had your choice of one of these Indian plaques which one would you choose? And would you be willing to pay more for example #3, than you would example #1?

Photo 3

The following Moose plaques represent yet another example of two plaques from the same mold, each decorated differently with varying degrees of art work and color variations. Study them carefully. Can you find the differences?

Chapter Three

Photographing Nippon A Simple Method

Polly Frye

Photographing china and porcelain does not have to be complex requiring lots of lights and props. You can have nice photographs of a collection with this simple method.

You should have a single lens reflex 35 mm camera. This will enable you to look through the lens and see exactly what you are recording on the film. There are many good 35 mm cameras on the market with automatic or manual exposure and focus. You want complete control over your exposures.

There is one essential requirement, get a GOOD LENS (I suggest a 52mm lens, for example). The body of the camera is not so important, but a good sharp lens that will focus down to at least two feet is a must in order to show detail on individual pieces. For very small pieces you need to get closer. You may be able to get detail without the cost of another expensive lens by obtaining a +2 or +3 close-up filter to put in front of your lens.

Another valuable piece of equipment is a tripod which prevents the camera from moving when the shutter is snapped. Make sure it is a sturdy tripod strong enough to hold your camera and a zoom lens.

A lens shade serves two purposes: it protects your lens and helps to keep light flare off of the lens. Be prepared to spend a minimum of $400.00 for a good quality camera, lens and lens shade.

If you photograph indoors, you will need a light source. Lights which flash create spots that you can not control. You may select two photo flood lights on stands, yet these do not always eliminate the hot spots, especially on highly glazed pieces.

Before you start to make photographs of your collection, you must decided which type of film to use. Print film is good and slides can be made from the negatives very successfully. However, prints made from slide film are not of the best quality. Choose a film with speeds of 100 or 200. You should not use film with a speed faster than 200. If you want two photos of each of your exposures, order two sets of prints when you have the film developed. It costs less to get two at the beginning than to reorder another set later, and in most cases first-run prints are better quality.

(You are saying to yourself, what about this simple way of photographing my collection?)

The best light source you can find is the sun. Open shade or an overcast day will give you a soft, even light. On a sturdy table, have several blocks of wood or cardboard boxes on hand to form pedestals. These can be placed under the cloth or paper you use as a background.

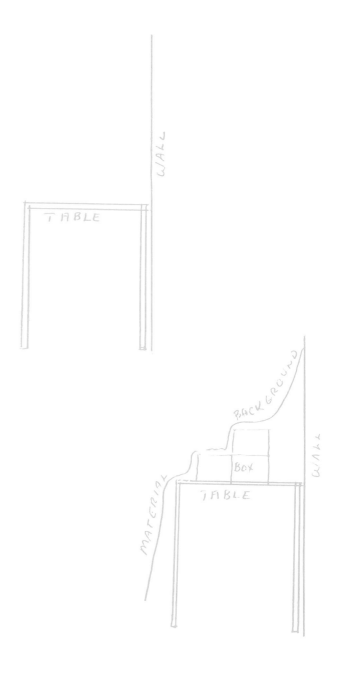

You must have the proper background for best results. Solid white or solid black, depending on the pieces to be photographed, give contrast between the object and the background. Photograph light-colored pieces on the black and darker pieces on white. Seamless background paper is available in many colors but you can certainly obtain excellent results with just black and white. Fabric backgrounds can be used very successfully if it does not have a shiny surface and is wrinkle free. This is very important. Felt and the back of velveteen works well. Fasten the background to a vertical surface (wall or side of the house) and run it down, across the table, and over the edge. By having one continuous strip, you have no distracting division line across the background of your photograph.

Look though your camera to select the best view. Sometimes lowering or raising the camera can show your piece to better advantage. Photograph sets all in one photograph, but don't try to show too many pieces in one photograph. You can't do justice to the detail unless you enlarge the photograph.

When you take your photographs inside, during daylight hours, place the table and background set-up described earlier near a window not in direct sunlight. Have the window light come across the items to be photographed from the side, and on the opposite side set up a large piece of white paper, posterboard will do. This serves as a reflector to throw light back into the shadow side of your items.

There is one more important point that I would like to make. Select a good photo lab to develop your film. Cheap processing does not always produce the results that your exposures deserve. Off color photographs can be the result of improper printing and many times the average persons thinks the problems is his fault and this may not be true. If you deal with the same lab you should be able to establish a good working relationship that will prove to be very beneficial to you and the lab as you buy your film and supplies.

You invest money in your collection and want photographs of it, you must invest in a good camera and lens to have good photographs.

Chapter Four
Advertising Items

Advertising and promotional items were produced to advertise and promote sales for different companies and products. In a effort to present their product to the customer in the fiercely competitive advertising world, these items contained catchy slogans, familiar slogans, or the company's logo. Originally these items were given away or sold inexpensively as premiums for purchasing the advertised product. They were purchased though mail order catalogs, grocery stores, gift shops, and dime stores.

These advertising goods were produced of lesser quality porcelain with little care given to the actual art work. Many advertising items were decorated with decals.

Advertising items are equally popular today as during the Nippon era, and many of the Nippon-marked advertising items are now sought after by advertising collectors and Nippon collectors alike.

A white porcelain rolling pin has advertising reading "We use Royal Household Flour, Canada's Best Flour." One thousand of these rolling pins were produced in Germany just prior to World War I, and marked with the backstamp "Made in Germany." When they were ready to be released as a flour premium, World War I broke out making anything marked "Made In Germany" undesirable. The first thousand rolling pins were destroyed, and new rolling pins were produced by Japanese potters with strict instructions that they be identical to the original. The Japanese complied so precisely that the new rolling pins boar the original "Made In Germany" backstamp. These rolling pins were again unusuable and destroyed. On the third order, the Japanese used their own Nippon backstamp.

Nippon items can be found with paper labels attached to them that read "Complements of the Morimura Brothers" and a date.

This most unique advertising tray is 4½" W. x 5½" H. and was probably used as a calling card tray. The scene depicts Japanese women hand-painting china chocolate sets, tea sets, and bowls. On the right you can see "The compliments of the Morimura Bros. New York." And if you look very carefully on the left at the top of the Pagoda you will find 1907 etched into the window pane. This piece in unmarked but unmistakenly Nippon. Very rare. Collection of Roger Zeefe.

Pedestal based compote 5" H. Business section from Seattle, Washington. SNB. Collections of Jess Berry and Gary Graves.

Whiskey jug 6½" H. Advertising item for "E.M. Higgins Old Velvet." M-in-wreath mark. Collection of Bartley and Catherine Casteel.

Bowl 8" W. Magenta m-in-wreath mark. Collection of Bartley and Catherine Casteel.

Chapter Five
Studio Items

Some Nippon items were imported to the United States as blanks. These blank bodies were unadorned except for the country of origin stamped on the backs or bottoms. Their decoration, by U.S. firms, is non-characteristic of Nippon.

In the 1880s, small craft guilds and art studios spread across the United States and United Kingdom. Many of these guilds were devoted to the design of pottery items as well as to perfecting the glazes. Vocational education for women was favored at that time. Women with an appreciation for the arts created a market for items made in the arts and craft schools.

From about 1880 to 1915, china painting came into vogue for the ladies of the day. For profit and to fill leisure time, women sought to learn decorating techniques. Small local studios opened up and china and pottery blanks were imported for decoration here. One company, well-known for this practice, was the Pickard China Company founded in 1897 in Chicago, Illinois. This decorating studio imported blanks from European manufacturers. Some of the early pieces bear the backstamps of these companies as well as Pickard.

The Spicer Studios, which operated in Akron Ohio from 1885 to 1910, was another well-known importer of European blanks. At this decoratinq school students in the china and porcelain paintinq classes were required to put the name "Spicer Studio" on their objects. The artists also signed items which they painted.

Other well-known United States companies that imported blanks include: Louis Wolf and Co., with studios in Boston, Mass. and New York City, Jonroth Studio, Royal Draqon Nippon Studio, and V Nippon from Scranton, Pa. James Studio China.

Most of the artist-signed Nippon items, which bear only the Nippon mark, were decorated at one of these studios and not in Japan.

Examples of Pickard Company decorated vases. They are marked Noritake/Nippon and "hand-painted Pickard China." Left vase 5½" H. artist signed "Falatke," Right Vase 7" H. artist signed "Challinor." Collection of Bob and Flora Wilson.

Mark S1

Gloria L.W. & Co. hand-painted Nippon. (Louis Wolf and Company, Boston, Mass. & N.Y.C.) Green.

Mark S6

Marks S2 and S3

Louis Wolf and Company, Boston Mass. and N.Y.C.

Mark S4

The Jonroth Studios hand-painted Nippon. Circa 1900. Magenta.

Mark S7

Mark S5

L.F.H. crown, hand-painted Nippon.

Mark S8

Mark S9

Nippon items which were decorated by Pickard. Mark #S6 Pickard etched china, Noritake Nippon Pickard mark is in black, Noritake/Nippon is blue, 1906. Mark #S7 Hand-painted Pickard china, gold. Mark #S8 Hand-painted Pickard China, Noritake Nippon, Pickard mark in black, Noritake Nippon in magenta. Mark #S9 Pickard gold leaf and blue Noritake/Nippon.

Mark S13

Kenilworth Studios. Blue. Nippon was produced at numerous little cottage industry locations throughout Japan, and because of their small size there is not a verifiable account of what was produced where or exactly when and by whom. Simply because there was not manpower or time enough to keep as accurate records as a larger company. Furthermore the records that were kept, have long since vanished. Research on the dating of these backstamps has turned up nothing except for the fact that they were produced in Japan during the Nippon Era 1891-1921.

Mark S10

Royal Dragon Nippon Studio hand-painted.

Mark S14

V Nippon, Scranton, Pennsylvania

Mark S11

Spicer Studio Akron Ohio Nippon. 1885-1915 found in brown.

Mark S15

James Studio China logo used in conjunction with Crown Nippon mark.

Mark S12

Studio hand-painted Nippon. Olive green.

Chapter Six
Portraits

Some of the most popular Nippon pieces are decorated with elaborate Victorian designs. The classical Nippon portrait pieces feature graceful shapes, lavishly decorated with gold overlay designs. They are richly enhanced with multi-colored enamel trim, shaped and colored to simulate jewels and an abundance of gold beading. The portraits are found in center medallions on the fronts of pieces edged in gold with gold beading. The reverse side of the medallion in almost all instances is floral rather than portraiture. Only cobalt portrait items have a scenic background.

It should be noted that Japanese artist could not paint a U.S. face. So a large percentage of Nippon portraits were applied as decals. This form of transfer decorating is a process whereby a design is made on a tissue-paper-thin print and applied to the porcelain surface. On these, only the borders and other decorating are actually done by hand. A few portraits on Nippon are completely hand-painted. To identify the decorating process, examine the object closely with a magnifying glass. If you see brush strokes or irregular lines, the object has been hand-painted. If you see a uniform series of dots or lines, the object has been decorated by decal.

All the Nippon decals were imported from Europe. They were copies of European companies' decals, including those used on porcelain objects which bear the backstamps of R.S. Prussia, Royal Vienna, E.S. Germany and others. The Noritake Company recently verified that in addition to decals, the blank bodies (or molds) themselves were also imported from Limoges, France and then decorated in Japan for export to the United States.

Hand-painted portraits are a Nippon rarity and generally these portraits depict common women. Painted portraits represent care-free, full figures of frivolous women.

The majority of Nippon portraits have the maple leaf backstamp.

Noritake officials confirm that the maple maple leaf mark is the oldest recorded Nippon mark with production beginning in 1891 by the Morimura Brothers.

It is not known when the maple leaf backstamp was last used. It is assumed that production of the maple leaf mark ended in 1911. At this time the registration and introduction of the Morimura Brothers M-in-wreath mark was implemented. The "M" represents Morimura and the wreath was designed from the Morimuras family crest. There is a dramatic difference in styles between Nippon portraits bearing the maple leaf mark and Nippon portraits bearing the M-in-wreath mark.

The Nippon portraits with the maple leaf mark are primarily women. Other subjects include Royal families, famous people based on paintings by renowned artists, Indian chiefs, ladies of the theatre, and typical people of that historical era.

The later Nippon portraits with the M-in-wreath backstamp are different as they display Art Nouveau styles. As the Victorian Era was winding down, the Art Nouveau era awakened. With this dawn of a new stylistic era, the techniques of enameling and moriage trims on Nippon came into vogue. More masculine Nippon portraits bear the M-in-wreath mark on objects favored by men like mugs, steins, wine jugs and

who was risque for a lady of that era. Her full name was Jeanne Francoise Juliette Adelaide Bernard. At fifteen she married a forty-two year old wealthy banker who was madly in love with her exquisite beauty. She delighted his eyes, and his vanity also. She flirted and charmed everyone at her famous "salons" where she entertained the important social and political figures of the time. He treated her as a pampered daughter and their relationship supposedly remained platonic for the duration of their 35 years of marriage.

Countess Anna Potocka (1776-1867), born Anna Tyckiewiez, was a Polish writer. Her memoirs are valuable as historical source material, covering the period from 1794-1820 and giving accounts of Napoleon's stay in Warsaw (1806-1807).

Marie Antoinette (1755-1793) was Queen of France and wife of King Louis XVI. As daughter of Maria Theresa of Austria, she sought Austria's aid against French Revolutionaries and counseled King Louis XVI in attempting the flight from France in 1791. Imprisoned with the King and their children, she was found guilty of treason and guillotined October 16, 1793. Her personal charm, a naive ignorance of practical life, extravagance, and frank, courageous honesty contributed to her unpopularity at court with the French people. When she was told that a revolution was in the air because the people had no bread, she is said to have replied, "Why don't they eat cake?"

Josephine de Beauharnais (1763-1814) was the beloved wife of Napoleon Bonaparte, one of French history's most prominent figures. As the daughter of a French planter in Martinique, West Indies, she was crowned empress of France at Napoleon's coronation on December 2, 1804. Napoleon divorced her in 1809.

Queen Victoria (1819-1901) was Queen of the United Kingdom and Empress of India. Her long reign included the industrial revolution and represents a period of English literature. In June of 1856, she instituted the Victoria Cross for acts of conspicuous valor in war, decorating the first recipients of the award herself.

Duchess Montpensier (1627-1693) was the French princess known in her life and remembered as La Grande Demoiselle.

The writer, Marie Therese Artner (1772-1829), wrote under the non de plum: Theone. In 1806, she published a book of selected poems and in 1818, wrote another called Field Flowers Gathered on the Plains of Hungary. She also was a dramatist. She had contact with and entertained many writers of note in her time.

Other Nippon portraits depict elegantly dressed, full-figured Victorian ladies in gardens or open meadows. These transfers are always found on a robin's-egg blue or pale turquoise background with clusters of gold beading. One shows a lady seated, while a second is standing holding a twig in her outstretched hand, awaiting the landing of a bird seen in the background. Another portrait also shows one lady seated, but the standing lady is bending, offering the seated lady a bird sitting on a twig. It is thought that this too could be attributed to the paintings done by Madame Lebrun. "La Paix Quiramene L'Abondunce" or "Peace bringing Back Abundance," the modern equivalent of "Faith Hope and Charity." Allegorically, the offering a bird on a twig is seen as an offering of peace; the outstretched twig in

humidors. They replaced delicate, fine feminine items such as vases, bowls and plaques of the Victorian era. The masculine items were decorated with men, dogs, monks, fat jolly old men, and cartoon art designs.

The decal portraits bearing the maple leaf mark depict easily identifiable women of that era, often members of European royal courts such as Madame Lebrun, Queen Louise, Queen Marie Antoinette, The Countess Anna Potocka, Madame Recamier, Josephine de Beauharnais, Queen Victoria, and The Dutchess Montpensier. They usually were copies of portraits by French artists. These women were idealized to the public of their time.

Queen Louise of Prussia (1776-1810) was born Louise of Mecklenburg-Strelitz. She ruled Prussia with her husband King Frederick William III from 1797 to 1810. She bore ten children during the seventeen happy years of her married life. Beauty, generosity, and courage in the face of trouble made her popular with her people. She reigned during the time of Napoleon's attacks on Prussia. After Prussian defeats at the battles of Jena and Friedland, she personally appealed to Napoleon to spare her country, but was unsuccessful.

Madame Lebrun (1755-1842) was a famous French artist. Born Marie Louise Elizabeth Virgée, her maiden name, Virgée, is usually included in identifying her work. It has been said that she secured more social triumphs and made fewer enemies than any other prominent person of her time. She accomplished this during one of the most troublous periods of French history, and her private life was not free from unpleasantness. She was a very successful court painter under the French King Louis XVI, and a favorite artist of Queen Marie Antoinette. She painted many portraits of the Queen and other beautiful women of the era. Today, her prestigious works hang in the Art galleries of Italy, Germany, Austria, Russia, France and England. Madame Lebrun can be found in two different views on Nippon portraits. The most frequent views show her with a white ribbon in her hair. The other view shows her wearing a white cap with a white ruffle around her neck.

Madame Recamier (1777-1849) was a French beauty

hand, indicates anticipation for peace.

"The Four Seasons" has been a popular theme of decoration for generations. The Nippon portraits with Cobalt blue backgrounds are another representation of the four seasons. The ladies hold seasonal flowers such as chrysanthemums for autumn and roses for summer. Each of the ladies has flowers in her hair, a single flower in one hand and a bouquet of flowers in the other. Two of these ladies have large bouquets in their right arms and two feature the bouquets in their left arms. Also, two bouquets are held in vases and two are shown as fresh bouquets with long stems.

All of the following items are marked with the Maple leaf mark.

Hand-painted pair of vases 12½" H. Maple leaf mark.

Covered urn 15½" H. Heavy enameled jewels. Queen Louise.

Vase 14¼" H. Queen Louise. Collections of Jess Berry and Gary Graves.

Queen Louise

Plate 9¾" W.

Bolted urn 13¼" H. Plate 9¾" W.

Covered urn 10" H. Moriage and jewels. Collection of Harold and Audrey Eklund.

Following pages:
Bolted covered urn 16" H. Rare. Madame Lebrun.

Ewer 12¼" H. Countess Anna Potocka.

Plate 10" W. Madame Lebrun.

Pair of vases 7½" H. Madame Récamier.

Pair of vases 8" H. Loop handles. This blank is frequently found decorated with portraits. Madame Lebrun.

Ewer 6¾" H. Madame Recámier.

Plate 10" W. Maple leaf mark. Vase 11" H. unmarked. Madame Recámier.

Countess Anna Potocka

Plate with scalloped edge and molded bows for handles 10" W. Scarce. Unmarked.

Pierced handled cake plate, coralene trim. Unmarked. Rare. This plate sold At the International Nippon Collectors Club Convention, in Harrisburg Pennsylvania, July 1990 for $3,500.

Vase 12" H.

Marie Antoinette

Covered urn with moriage trim 11" H. Rare. Covered urn red background. Rare. Collections of Jess Berry and Gary Graves.

10" Plate, green background, heavy red jewels. Scarce.

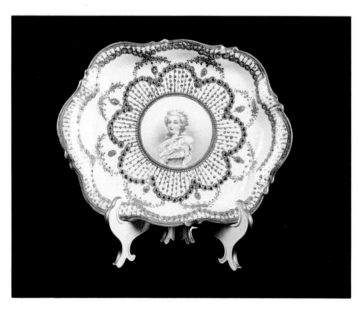

Tray 9" W. Enameled jewels. Scarce.

Melon ribbed body fancy handles vase 8½" H. Unmarked.

Plate 10" W. Josephine de Beauharnais.

Vase 8½" H. Duchess Montpeusier.

Vase 8½" H. Marie Therese Artner.

Plate 10" W. Queen Victoria. Collection of Harold and Audrey Eklund.

Vase 10" H.

Vase 5¾" H.

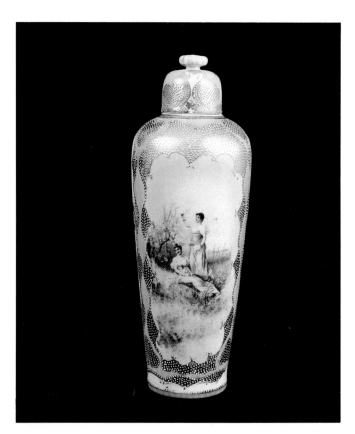

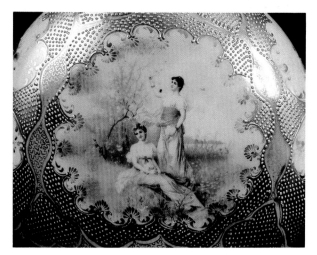

Close up of scene.

La Paix Quiramene L' Abondance, or Peace bringing back abundance the modern equivalent of Faith, Hope, and Charity.

Footed ewer 10" H.

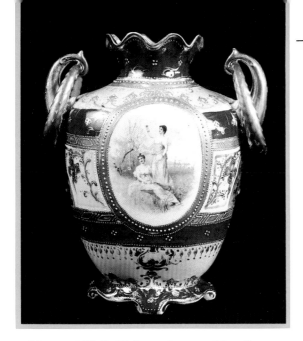

Vase 9½" H. Ruffled top, ring pretzel handles.

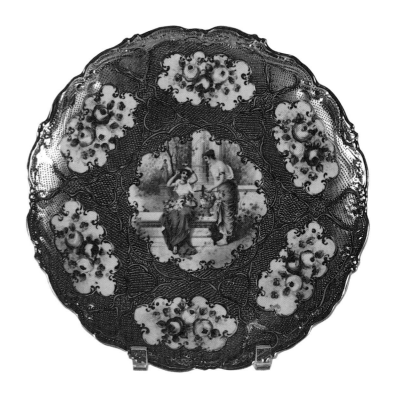

Plate 12⅜" W. Collection of Harold and Audrey Eklund.

Vase 8" x 8". Unmarked.

This tea set is a combination of both scenes. Pot 8½" H. Cream 6½" H. sugar 6" H. Unmarked. Rare.

Cobalt Four Seasons

Four footed vase 7½" H.

Vase 5" H. Scarce.

Pair of vases 8" H. Center vase 4¾" H.

Vase 10½" H. 10" Plaque. Collection of George and Donna Avezzano.

Vase 7¾" H.

Vase 6" H.

"Lady with the Peacock." Vase 6" H. Coralene. Patent mark. Rare. Collection of Bob and Flora Wilson.

"Lady with the Doves." Tankard 13¾" H. Rare.

"Lady with the Peacock" 5½" H. Ruffled neck, ring pretzel handles.

Vase 12" H. Lady with the Peacock. This blank is found frequently with portrait decoration.

Covered urn 14¼" H. One of the four seasons girls "summer." Rare.

Footed scalloped edged, pierced handled dish 3¼" H. x 6½" W.

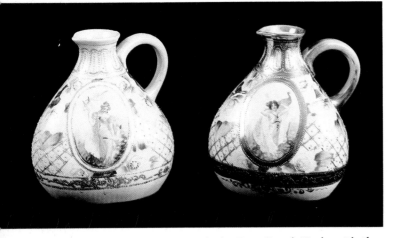

Pair of jugs 8" H. "Lady with the Doves" and "Lady with the Peacock."

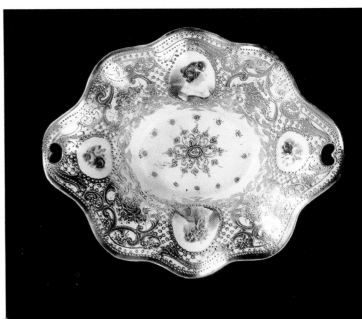

Footed covered box 7" x 7".

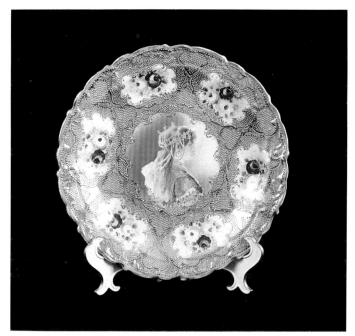

Plate 10½" W.

Plate 10½" H.

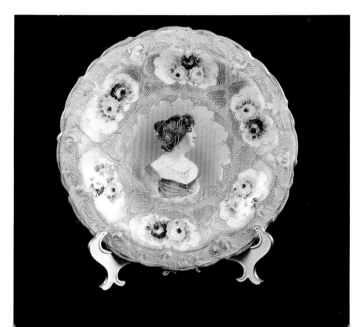

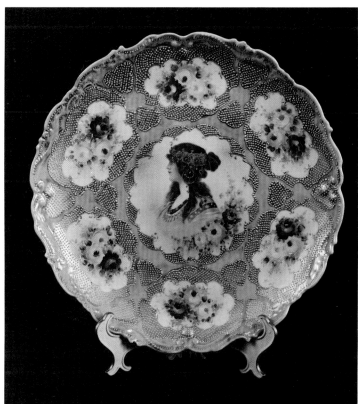

Plaque 12½" W.

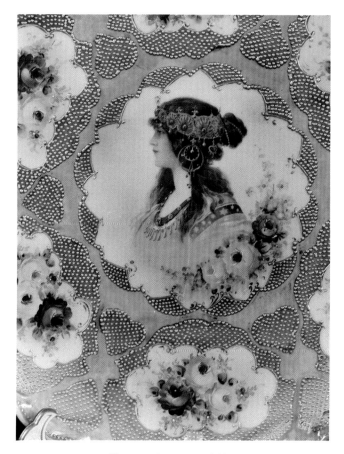

Close up of center medallion.

Vase 6" H. Ruffled top, ring pretzel handles.

Plate 10" W. Heavy enameled jewels.

Plate 8¾" W. Heavy enameled jewels. Scarce. Collection of Bob and Flora Wilson.

Plate 10" W. Heavy enameled jewels. Scarce. Collection of Polly Frye.

Trinket box, 2" H. x 3¼" W. Moriage trim.

Bolted urn 12¼" H.

Hanging hat pin holder or hanging vase 7". Rare.

Pair of plaques 9¾" W. Scarce.

Dresser set tray 12" x 9", footed hair receiver and covered powder box, covered trinket 2" x 2½", pedestal based pin dish 5" x 2½". Rare. Collection of Harold and Audrey Eklund.

Two footed hair receivers, covered trinket, and closed hat pin holder with rocking bottom.

Close up of pedestal based pin tray.

Three handled tooth pick holder.

Miniature covered trinket box 2"x 1¾". Lid has portrait of man in uniform and is titled "Admiral Togo" he was a Japanese captain who helped defeat the Russian fleet during the Russo-Japan War of 1904. Unmarked. Collection of Jerry and Linda Cox.

Footed creamer 4" H., sugar bowl with lid 6" H.

Napoleon Bonaparte (1769-1821) plate 6½" W. Rising sun mark. Scarce.

Miniature covered trinket box 1½" x 2". Moriage trim.

Monk humidor 7" H. This is not the original lid.

Humidor 7½" H. Moriage and jewels trim.
Collection of Stanley Jones.

Back and side profile 9½" W. plaque.

The Cardinals "red hat" was made part of the
official vestments in 1245 "In token of their
being ready to lay down their life for the gospel."
Nippon items shown with the Cardinal portrait
can be found in these two views and on very few
items, he can also be found on a tankard and
mugs.

Full face view plaque 9½" W. Collection of
Frank and Betty Bryson.

Monk mug 5½" H. M-in-wreath mark.

Stein 7½" H. Enameled trim. M-in-wreath mark. Collection of Roger Zeefe.

Stein 7½" H. Enameled trim. M-in-wreath mark. Collection of Roger Zeefe.

"Cartoon Art" stein 7½" H. Collection of Roger Zeefe.

Monk wine jug 9½" H.

Chapter Seven
Urns and Covered Urns

A bolted urn, is actually two pieces of porcelain that are physically bolted together with a threaded rod and nut to secure the two items together. The bolting process is used when the pedestal base has a narrow extension leading to the vase itself. The top heavy object requires a separate base in order that it does not become unsymmetrical in the wet mold stage.

Bolted, covered urn 17½" H. Maple leaf mark. Collection of Rolfes and Virginia Hensley.

Covered Urn 12½" H. Seahorse handles. Blue Maple leaf mark.

Bolted, covered Urn 15¾" H. Maple leaf mark. Collections of Jess Berry and Gary Graves.

Bolted, covered urn 16" H. Ramshead handles. M-in-wreath mark. Collection of George and Donna Avezzano.

Bolted, covered urn 13¼" H. Royal Kinran mark. Collections of Jess Berry and Gary Graves.

Pair of Bolted covered urns 18½" H. Maple leaf mark.

Covered urn 14" H. Chrysanthemums are said to promote good health and longevity. Maple leaf mark. Collection of Stanley Jones.

Covered urn 13½″ H. Blue Maple leaf mark. Collection of Bob and Flora Wilson.

Covered urn 13¼" H. Royal Moriye mark. Collection of Wayland and Brenda Horton.

Covered urn 10¾" H. Maple leaf mark. Collection of Bob and Floral Wilson.

Bolted covered urn 15½" H. M-in-wreath mark. Collection of Bob and Flora Wilson.

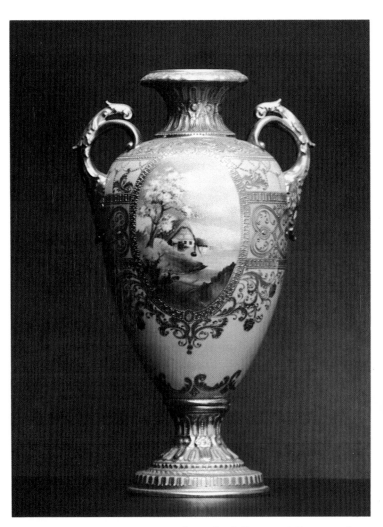

Bolted urn 16" H. M-in-wreath mark. Collection of George and Donna Avezzano.

Bolted urn 14½" H. M-in-wreath mark.

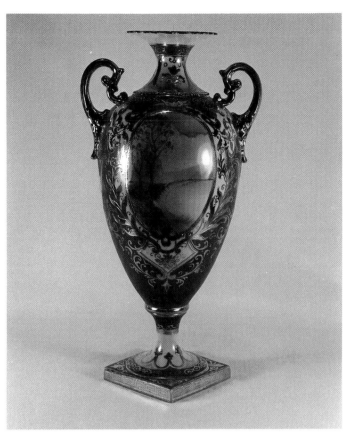

Bolted urn 15½" H. Maple leaf mark. Collection of Harold and Audrey Eklund.

Pair of bolted urns 16¾" H. M-in-wreath mark. Collection of George and Donna Avezzano.

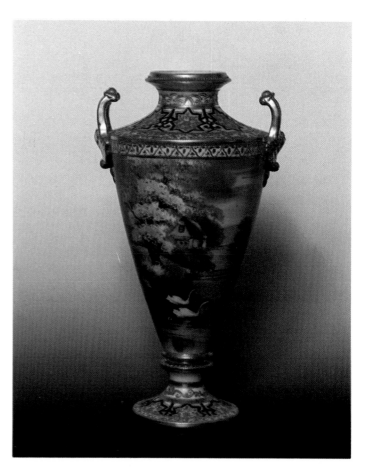

Bolted urn ll" H. Rams head handles. Collection of George and Donna Avezzano.

Bolted urn 13¾" H. Urn 14¾" H. Urn 13½" H. Maple leaf mark. Collection of George and Donna Avezzano.

Bolted urn 14½" H. M-in-wreath mark. Collection of Lewis Longest Jr., FP, CPP.

Chapter Eight
Groups

Egyptian Motif. Top row: Pair of triangular candlesticks 8" H., Trivet 6½" W., Bowl 8" W., Trivet 6½" W. All green M-in-wreath mark. Collections of Jess Berry and Gary Graves.

Egyptian motif. Top row: humidor 4¼" H. front view. Ashtray 4" W., Humidor, reverse side. Bottom row: Egyptian princess ashtrays 4¼" W., Humidor 4¾" H. Green M-in-wreath mark. Collections of Jess Berry and Gary Graves.

Ruins Scene, with white enameled flowers, vase 11¾" H. M-in-wreath mark. Collections of Jess Berry and Gary Graves.

Ruins Scene. Bowl 8½" W. Plaque 10" W. Vase 9" H. Private collection.

Ruins Scene, with white enameled flowers. Top plaque 10" W. Center Vase 8½" H. Bottom Vase 8½" H., Covered box 7" W. Vase 9½" H. All M-in-wreath. Collections of Jess Berry and Gary Graves.

Christmas deer, pair of plaques, 10" W. Green Maple leaf mark. Collections of Jess Berry and Gary Graves.

Christmas deer Tankard Set with Moriage flowers and trim.
Tankard 11" H., Mugs 4¾" H. M-in-wreath mark. Collections of
Jess Berry and Gary Graves.

Christmas deer. Wine jug with original wicker basket 9½" H. Three
handled humidor 6" H. wine jug original wicker basket 8" H.
M-in-wreath. Collections of Jess Berry and Gary Graves.

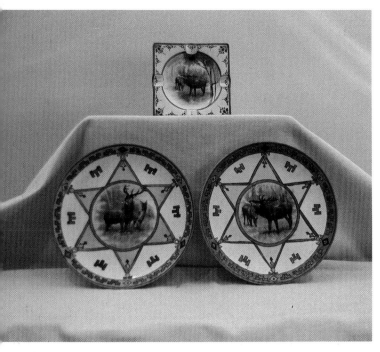

Double Moose in Star. Ashtray 5½" W. Plaques 8¾" W. Green M-in-wreath mark. Collections of Jess Berry and Gary Graves.

Humidor 4" H. M-in-wreath mark. Dorland/Pegg collection.

Plaques 7¾" W. M-in-wreath mark. Dorland/Pegg collection.

Birds such as swans, sea gulls, and pheasants can be found on many Nippon items.

Photo #469 B Plaque, 11" W. Maple leaf mark. Collection of Ted and Nita Ensign.

Fisherman and Cart vase 12½" H. Dorland/Pegg collection.

Fisherman and Cart plaque 11" W. M-in-wreath mark. Private collection.

Vase 11¼" H. Gold overlay design, mountain and lake scene, ribbon handles, top and bottom of slightly molded-in-relief design. Maple leaf mark.

Plaque 10" W., Covered hat pin holder 5" H. Vase 9½" H.

Candle stick, 8" H. Maple leaf mark.

Cylinder shape vase 15" H. Maple leaf mark. Collection of Rolfes & Virginia Hensley.

Mountain and lake scene vase 6½" H. Maple leaf mark.

Bolted urn 13" H. Plaque 11" W. Blue Maple leaf mark.

Plaque, 10" W.

Vase 5½" H., Vase 8½" H., Ring pretzel handles, ruffled top opening. M-in-wreath mark. Collection of Ted and Nita Ensign.

Pierced handled, scalloped edge, stone bridge scene cake plate 12½" W. Footed stone bridge scene dish.

Windmill scene, left to right: Vase 5½" H., Mug 5½" H., Vase 7½" H. Vase 8" H. M-in-wreath mark. Collection of George & Doris Myers.

Banquet Punch set. 13" H. punch bowl sits on pedestal base. 6 matching pedestal based cups. M-in-wreath mark. Collection of Rolfes and Virginia Hensley.

Aqua beaded rose, left to right: Vase, 7" H. Maple leaf mark. Vase 4½" H. Royal Kinran mark. Vase, 9" H. Maple leaf mark. Vase, 5" H. Dowsie Nippon mark.

Aqua beaded rose pattern. Charger, 12¼" W. Salt and pepper shakers, 2" H., unmarked. Three handled toothpick. Maple leaf mark. Tankard, Oriental China mark. Private collection.

Aqua beaded rose. Chocolate Pot, 10" H. Oriental China mark. Pedestal-base cream and sugar, 5¼" H. Private collection.

Gold beaded, scalloped-edge nappy. 7" W. Plate 7" W. Unmarked. Collection of Wayland and Brenda Horton.

Aqua beaded rose ewer, 4½" H. x 7¾" W. Phil and Jeanne Fernkes collection.

Aqua beaded rose. Three handled spooner 5" H. x 4¼" W. Oriental china mark. Collection of George and Doris Myers.

Gold beaded three-piece pedestal-base tea set. pot, 6¼" H. Cream and sugar, 5¾" H. Unmarked. Collection of Wayland and Brenda Horton.

Combination of aqua and gold beading. Heart-shaped trinket box, 2¾" W. Vase with elephant handles, 6" H. Vase 3½" H. Maple leaf mark.

Cream and sugar. Maple leaf mark. Collection of Wayland and Brenda Horton.

Combination of aqua and gold beading covered urn 10" H. Maple leaf mark. Bob and Flora Wilson collection.

Orchids outlined in gold with jewels. Vase 9½" H. Ring pretzel handles, ruffled top. Pitcher 7¾" H. Blue Maple leaf mark.

Pair of basket vases 8¾" H. Maple leaf mark. Collection of Wayland and Brenda Horton.

Orchids outlined in gold. Scalloped edge bowl 11" W. M-in-wreath mark. Collection of Cathy Keys.

"Cowboy in Silhouette" Vase 8" H. M-in-wreath mark. Cigarette box, 5½" W. M-in-wreath mark. Rita and Bob Gillis collection.

Indian and Canoe scene. Vase, 15" H. Footed and mellon ribbed cracker jar. Vase, 7¼" H. M-in-wreath mark.

"Dancing Peasants" scene. Stein, 7" H. M-in-wreath mark.

"Dancing Peasants" scene. Loving cup, 7" H. M-in-wreath mark.

"Dancing Peasants" Humidor, 7" H. M-in-wreath mark.

"Dancing Peasants" scene. Vase, 9½" H. M-in-wreath mark.

Chapter Nine

Moriage

Moriage (pronounced Mor-ee-ah-ga) is an art technique used to decorate Japanese ceramics (porcelain, soft-paste wares and pottery) that were produced for export to the United States and United Kingdom during the Nippon Era (1891-1921).

Moriage is an Oriental word which translates loosely "to pile up" and refers to applied relief motifs affixed to ceramic works to create a design with a three-dimensional quality.

The raised decoration was applied before firing in one of three ways: 1) slip was rolled and shaped, then put manually on the object in one or more layers, with thickness and shape depending on the desired design, 2) tubing or slip trailing was applied from a tube in a manner similar to that used today to decorate cakes, 3) slip was reduced to a liquid and applied with a brush—the Japanese word for this is *Hankeme*.

The Moriage technique is an old technique. Since the mid-1700s, both Japanese and Chinese porcelain and pottery factories produced Moriage wares for domestic use. However, Japanese exportation of these wares began and ended with the Nippon era.

Moriage designs are varied and innumerable. They range from an all-over lacy effect to border trimmings; there are birds, animals, plum and wheat patterns, as well as the jeweled-eyed dragon pattern. And just as there are seemingly endless designs, these designs appear on a large variety of objects—many of which reflect the lifestyles of fashionable American at the turn of the century.

Before World War I, genteel ladies in England and America gathered regularly for afternoon tea. The hostess's tea set was her status symbol, so it's not surprising that elaborate Moriage tea pots, creamers, sugar bowls, tea strainers, cups, saucers, luncheon plates, cookie and cracker jars were highly sought after. A 1908 Butler Brothers catalog features a very fancy Moriage tea pot, creamer, sugar bowl and two cups and saucers priced at $1.95. While this was expensive at the time (lesser tea sets sold for 96 cents, and non-Moriage cups and saucers in the catalog were priced at 89 cents per dozen) it is a far cry from what these pieces command today. A Moriage tea pot, creamer, sugar bowl, and three cups and saucers very much like those in the Butler Brothers catalog sold for $995 at a December, 1990 antique show in Indianapolis, Indiana. Single Moriage cups and saucers now bring from $25 to $125, depending on quality.

Tankard unusual all over decoration and unusual color combination. 13¼" H. unmarked. Collection of Jerry and Linda Cox.

Ladies' toiletries were also much in evidence in the late 1800s and early 1900s, and Moriage designs can be found on many powder boxes, hair receivers, hat pin holders, and perfume bottles. Complete dresser sets are rare. So too, are complete smoking sets, which include a tray, cigarette holder, match holder, and sometimes, a humidor. Other Moriage items include lamps, vases, covered urns, bowls and wall plaques.

Many Moriage items bear a variety of Nippon marks, which include the M-in-wreath, blue maple leaf, Oriental china Nippon, Pagoda, Royal Nishiki, and the Royal Moriye marks. Items bearing the Royal Moriye mark confuse some collectors. The word "Moriye" is the name of a company that produced Moriage decorated items. But an even larger amount of Moriage pieces are unmarked or are stamped with Oriental characters alone or enclosed in a square or circle; these characters designate the company of production. However, in the last 40 years, collectors acknowledge the credibility of the large amount of unmarked Moriage wares.

Collecting Hints: Though the Moriage technique was used to decorate soft-paste and pottery as well as porcelain wares, it is the porcelains that are most sought after by collectors. The quality of the art work and application of Moriage is noticeably finer and has greater detail on porcelain objects than on soft-paste or pottery objects. Nippon collectors generally prefer items bearing the Nippon backstamp.

The appreciation for items made with the Moriage technique is growing in leaps and bounds, for it is truly a lost art and prices have skyrocketed in the last five years.

Examples of slip trailing and heavy Moriage beading on pink marbleized background. Collection of Jerry and Linda Cox. All items rare.

Covered urn, 9¼" H. Unmarked.

Bolted covered urn, 18½" H. Unmarked.

Covered wine decanter, 14½" H. Unmarked.

Humidor, with figural squirrel Unmarked.

Center medallions of hand-painted pink and yellow roses, enhanced with heavy Moriage pine cones and leaves. Beaded trim on handles. Collection of Jerry and Linda Cox.

Ewer 7¼" H.

Vase 8" H.

Vase 13¼" H.

Cream and sugar 4″ H. Vase 9¼″ H. Royal Moriye mark.
Collection of Wayland and Brenda Horton.

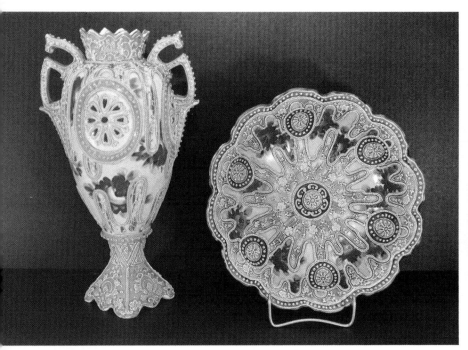

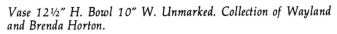

Vase 12½″ H. Bowl 10″ W. Unmarked. Collection of Wayland
and Brenda Horton.

Vase 8¾″ H. Unmarked. Collection of Wayland and Brenda
Horton.

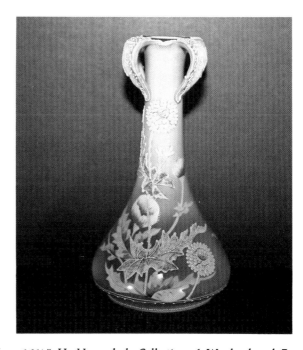

Vase 10½" H. Unmarked. Collection of Wayland and Brenda Horton.

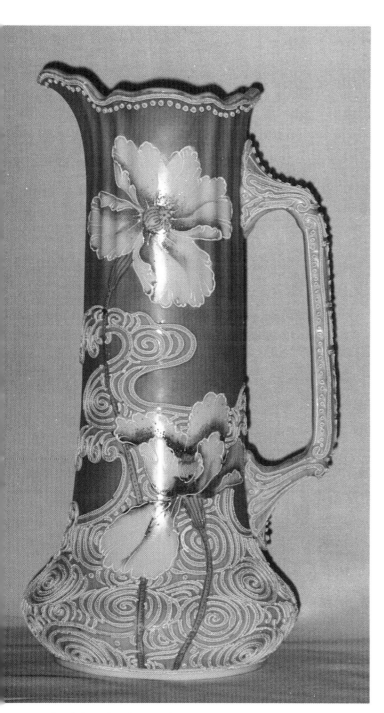

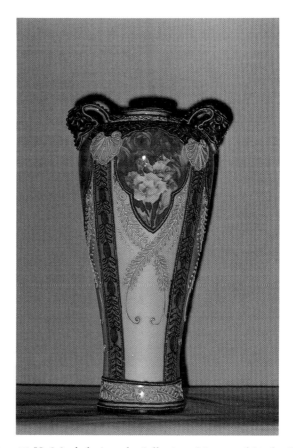

Vase 9" H. Maple leaf mark. Collection of Jerry and Linda Cox.

Tankard, large hand-painted flowers with Moriage trim. 13½" H. Oriental china mark.

Charger 13¼" W. Maple leaf mark. Collection of Bob and Flora Wilson.

14" H. Unmarked. Collection of Wayland and Brenda Horton.

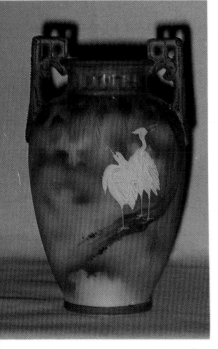 

One of the many different birds found on a variety of objects. These egrets, which is a species of the herons, are not readily found on Nippon objects. Vase 6½" H. Ewer 6" H. Green M-in-wreath mark. Collection of Jerry and Linda Cox.

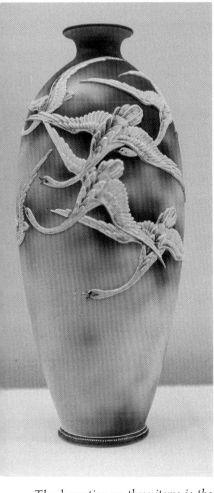

The Moriage snow geese are a favorite design with collectors. These graceful birds are most commonly painted on a pale robin's egg blue background that shades into a muted gray. Most of the Moriage items with flying geese decoration bear the blue Maple leaf mark.

The decoration on these items is the large snow geese only. Bottle vases: left 10½" H. right 8¾" H. Bottle vase 14¼" H. Collections of Jess Berry and Gary Graves.

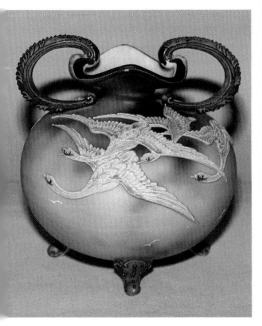

These vases also show the large Moriage snow geese with tiny Moriage birds in flight. 7½" H. 6½" H. Basket vase 8¾" H.

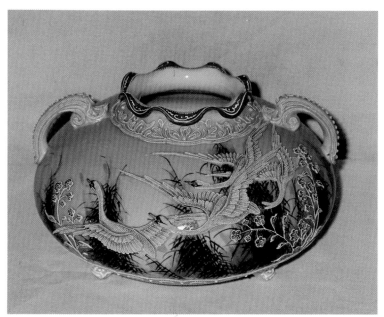

These geese can also be found on items with an all robin's egg blue background, and very few geese appear on this vivid multi-colored background. 8½" W. x 5" H. 7¼" H.

The majority of the snow geese, regardless of the background colors, fly from right to left. Rarely will you find an object that shows the geese flying from the left to right. 9" H. Vase, footed and mellon ribbed 8¼" H. Oriental China mark. Collection of Jerry and Linda Cox.

Examples of other Moriage birds that can be found.

Vase 7" H. Ring handles. Maple leaf mark. Collection of Jerry and Linda Cox.

Bottle vase 10¼" H. Collections of Jess Berry and Gary Graves.

Vase 8½" H. Blue Maple leaf mark. Collection of Jerry and Linda Cox.

Vase 9½" H. Collection of Jerry and Linda Cox.

Vase 9¾" H. Collection of Jerry and Linda Cox.

Vase 5¼" H. Stand up handles. M-in-wreath mark. Collection of Jerry and Linda Cox.

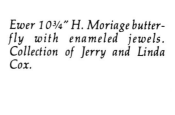

Ewer 10¾" H. Moriage butterfly with enameled jewels. Collection of Jerry and Linda Cox.

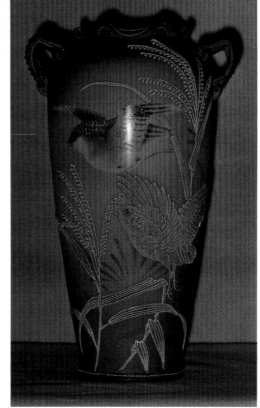

Vase 10¾" H. Maple leaf mark. Collection of Jerry and Linda Cox.

Vase 9" H. One painted and one Moriage bird. Maple leaf mark.

Crocus Vase 4½" H. Moriage butterfly with enameled jewels. Unmarked. Collection of Lewis Longest, Jr., FP, CPP.

Vase 7¼" H. Mark has been scratched off. Collection of Jerry and Linda Cox.

These are examples of the same mold decorated with different designs.

Vase 11½" H.

Covered urn 8" H.

Three twist handled vase 10" H.

Vase 11¼" H. Maple leaf mark.

Covered urn 8" H.

Three twist handled vase 10" H.
Royal Moriye mark.

Moriage jewel-eyed dragon. (also see molded-in-relief section)

Tankard set, Tankard 14" H. mugs 5½" H.
M-in-wreath mark. Collection of Wayne and
Mary Myers.

Ewers 6¾" H. 11½" H. 12" H. M-in-wreath
mark. Collection of Wayne and Mary Myers.

Vase 8½" H. Vase 11" H. Vase 11" H. M-in-wreath mark. Collection of Wayne & Mary Myers.

Loving cup vase 4¾" H. Vase 11½" H. Ferner 6¾" W. M-in-wreath mark. Collection of Wayne and Mary Myers.

Chocolate set, footed, and mellow ribbed, R.S. Prussia mold, Pot 12" H. Four cups and saucers, Maple leaf mark. Collection of Wayne and Mary Myers.

Dresser set, Tray 11½"
footed powder box, closed
hat pin holder, pedestal
based trinket, footed hair
receiver. M-in-wreath
mark. Collecion of Wayne
and Myers.

Demitasse after dinner coffee set.
Tray 12" W. Coffee Pot 6½"
H. Cream, sugar, six cups and
saucers. M-in-wreath mark.
Collection of Wayne and Mary
Myers.

Match holder 5" H. Humidor 7" H. M-in-wreath mark.
Collection of Wayne and Mary Myers.

Basket 5" H. Collection of Jerry and Linda Cox.

Ferner 10½" W. x 53/5" H. Collection of Jerry and Linda Cox.

Footed and mellon ribbed cracker jar 7½" H. M-in-wreath mark.
Collection of Wayne and Mary Myers.

*Aladdin shaped, pedestal based tea set. Pot 5½" H. Cream and sugar
5" H, six cups and saucers. M-in-wreath mark. Collection of Wayne
and Mary Myers.*

*Chocolate set, octagon shape. Pot 10"H., five cups and saucers.
M-in-wreath mark. Collection of Wayne and Mary Myers.*

Vase with Sea Horse handles 12" H. Very rare. Private Collection.

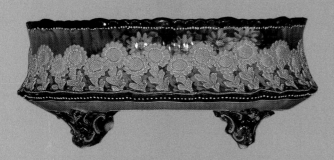

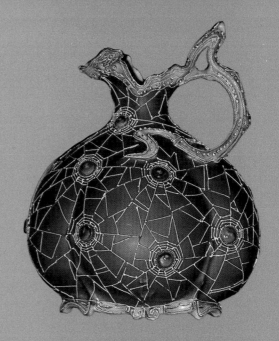

Ferner 3¾" H. x 8¾" W. Maple leaf mark. Collection of Jerry and Linda Cox.

Moriage spider webs with large jewels. Ewer 9" H. Maple leaf mark. Humidor 5¾" H. Collection of Jerry and Linda Cox.

Vase 6¼" H. Collection of Jerry and Linda Cox.

Bolted, covered urn 10½" H. Collection of Jerry and Linda Cox.

Ewer 3½" H. Unmarked. Collection of Jerry and Linda Cox.

Ewer 9¼" H. Unmarked. Collection of Jerry and Linda Cox.

Vase, molded-in-relief hand holding vase 12" H. Collection of Jerry and Linda Cox.

Vase 12" H. Collection of Jerry and Linda Cox.

Ewer 6¼" H. Collection of Jerry and Linda Cox.

Tea Pot 6½" H. Collection of Jerry and Linda Cox.

Tea Pot 6½" H. Collection of Jerry and Linda Cox.

Ewer 15" H. Unmarked. Collection of Jerry and Linda Cox.

Ewer 10¼" H. Collection of Jerry and Linda Cox.

Moriage Eagle with Sea Serpent handles 10" H. Very Rare.
Collection of Dorland/Pegg.

Chapter Ten
Coralene

From left to right. Vase 4¼" H. Vase 6" H. Vase 4¾" H. Miniature pitcher 4¼" H. Footed Vase 4¾" H. All have February 9, 1909 Patent mark. Collection of Lewis Longest Jr., FP, CPP.

The Coralene finish is easily recognized by iridescence over a design composed of tiny glass beads. This effect is achieved by firing small colorless glass beads on glass, porcelain or pottery bodies.

Several American and English companies have made glass Coralene since the 1800s and Japanese Coralene on china and porcelain was made for export to the United States and United Kingdom from the late 1890s to the post World War II era. The manufacturing process was perfected and patented in 1909 by Alban L. Rock, an American citizen living in Yokohama, Japan.

The background finish on most of these pieces is a matte glaze with soft shading of color. There are pieces with high glaze backgrounds.

The main components of the fusing substance were silicate of Albumen and flux to which was added a dry porcelain pigment and water. This mixture was applied to a predetermined design on the porcelain body in a wet state. Then, tiny, round, colorless and transparent beads were placed on top of the fusing mixture which held them in place. Great care had to be taken so that the coating of beads was uniform in order to obtain a smooth finish. The decorated piece was then fired in the usual manner so that the beads were permanently fixed to the body.

Although Coralene items were manufactured in Japan during the Nippon era, few bear the Nippon backstamp. However, Coralene items are included in many Nippon collections. Backstamps on Japanese Coralene include

"U.S. Patent, 912-171, Feb. 9, 1909" with the word "Japan." Number 16137 is a British Patent Office registration number. Some original pieces are marked, "Patent Applied for, 382-57" or "Patent Pending" without the word "Japan." The word "Kinran" can also be found, accompanied by Japanese characters and sometimes with the patent number. These marks are usually blue or magenta in color.

Many of the designs reflect Art Nouveau style. Colors are often vivid and unusual. The blanks are identical, or very similar to Nippon blanks.

A few pieces of Coralene are marked "RC Nippon" accompanied by a mark similar to the rising sun mark. These pieces lack the plushness of color and iridescence found on Japanese Coralene pieces. The shapes of the body are simple and without trim.

Collecting hint: On very close inspection, most Coralene items have minor amounts of beads missing from the tips of flowers, branches, wings, etc. Small amounts of missing beads are acceptable to collectors, without bearing on price. However, if a Coralene object has sections with chips in the finish or big sections of missing beads, its price should be lower than an object with no missing beads or damage.

REPRODUCTION ALERT: There are a small quantity of Coralene reproductions on the market, most on old glass bases. The beaded decoration on new Coralene has been fixed with glue, not a fired process, so the glass beads can be easily scratched off.

Vase 7" H. Patent mark. Collection of Lewis Longest Jr., FP, CPP.   *Vase 8" H. Patent mark. Collection of Lewis Longest Jr., FP, CPP.*

*Scenic Coralene items are scarce. Vase 9¼" H. Vase 6½" H. Patent
mark. Collection of Lewis Longest Jr., FP, CPP.*

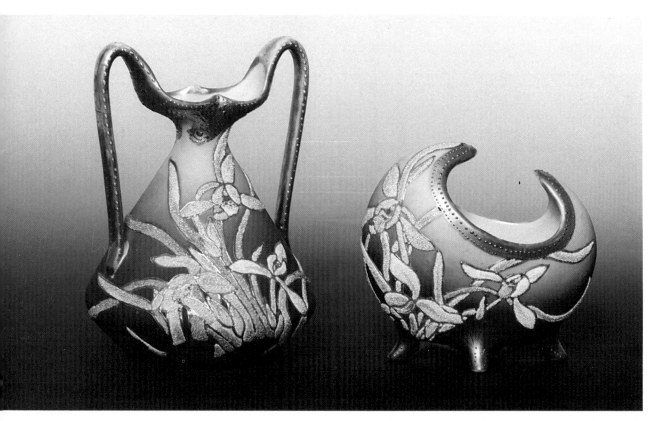

Vase 7" H. Unusual footed vase 5" H. Patent mark. Collection of Lewis Longest Jr., FP, CPP.

Vase 10" H. Background shades from turquoise to yellow to a pale pink. Elephant head handles. Patent mark. Collection of Lewis Longest Jr., FP, CPP.

Vase 9" H. Patent mark. Collection of Lewis Longest Jr., FP, CPP.

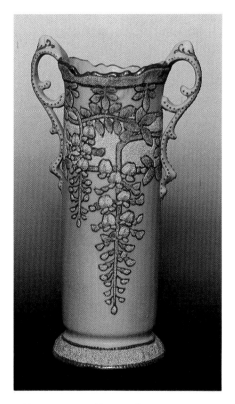

Vase, 11¼" H. Trailing Wisteria. Reticulated handles. Collection of Lewis Longest Jr., FP, CPP.

Vase 9" H. Patent mark. Collection of Lewis Longest Jr., FP, CPP.

Hat Pin Holder 4" H. Rare. Closed top and rocking bottom. Patent mark. Collection of Harold and Audrey Eklund.

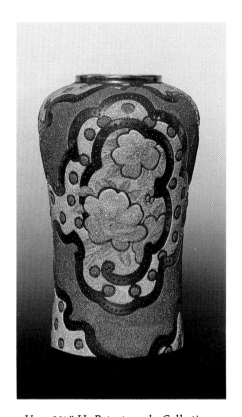

Vase 8½" H. Patent mark. Collection of Lewis Longest Jr., FP, CPP.

Vase 11" H. Patent mark. Collection of Lewis Longest Jr., FP, CPP.

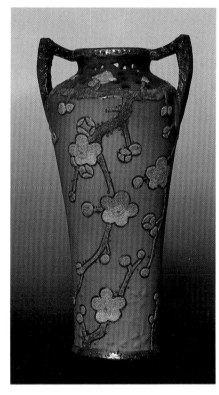

Vase 10" H. Collection of Lewis Longest Jr., FP, CPP.

*Chamberstick cobalt, unusual 2½" H. x 6¼" W. Patent mark.
Collection of Lewis Longest Jr., FP, CPP.*

*Vase 7¼" H. Daffodils. Patent mark. Collection of Lewis Longest
Jr., FP, CPP.*

*Footed basket, cobalt, rare 3½" H. x 4¾" W. Patent mark.
Collection of Harold and Audrey Eklund.*

*Pair of vases 9¾" tall, cobalt blue background. Patent mark.
Collection of Lewis Longest Jr., FP, CPP.*

*Ewer 10½" H. Notice the rare molded-in-relief gargole in neck of
ewer. Patent mark. Collection of Lewis Longest Jr., FP, CPP.*

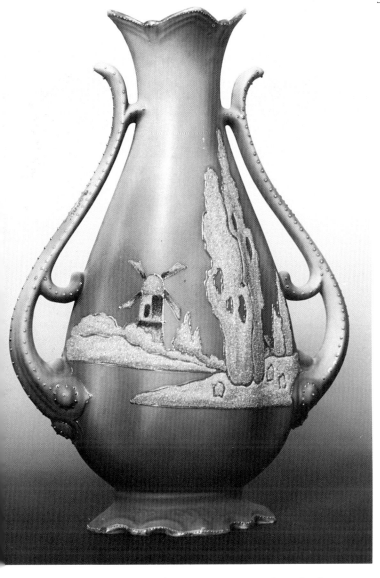

Vase 15". Bleeding hearts floral. Patent mark. Collection of Olin & Grace Harkleroad.

Vase 12" H. Scarce Coralene scenic of trees and windmill. Patent mark. Collection of Lewis Longest Jr., FP, CPP.

Vase 9¾" H. unusual elephant trunk rings at base. Tankard 13¼" H. Bolted Ewer 10½" H. Collection of George and Donna Avezzano.

Bolted, covered urn. 14" H. Patent mark.

Vase 4½" H. Vase 6¾" H. Vase 5" H. Patent mark.

Footed basket 3¾" H. x 5" W. Ewer 5¼" H. Cobalt vase 3¼" H. Patent mark.

Coralene vase 9" H. Patent mark. Polly Frye Collection.

Vase 7¾" H. Patent mark. Collection of Bill and Francile Mc Lain.

Vase 12" H. Collection of Bill and Francile Mc Lain.

Chapter Eleven

Wedgwood

These items are decorated in the classic Wedgwood blue and white manner. Against the classic blue background the white Wedgwood design was created by using the Moriage slip trailing method. Wet liquid clay formed the raised design. The sprigged on decorations were made with a thicker clay and applied by hand to form layers of decoration.

Pair of candlesticks 8" H. Collection of Bob and Flora Wilson.

Ferner, with molded-in-relief handles. 8½" W. x 4" H. Scarce. Collection of Bob and Flora Wilson.

Mug 5" H. Collection of Bob and Flora Wilson.

Classic Wedgwood designs are white on a darker blue background, here we find a example of "reversed" Wedgwood. The background color is a pale yellow and the Wedgwood designs are done in a pale but darker blue. Vase 6" H. Collection of Bob and Flora Wilson.

Classic blue and white Wedgwood, with hand-painted scenes. Cream and sugar, collection of Howard and Shirley Grubka. Vase 9" H. Wedgwood sprigged-on method used to decorate top of vase. Collection of Bob and Flora Wilson.

Top and bottom band of classic blue and white Wedgwood with large roses. Pair of candlesticks 6" H. Vase 5" H. Collection of Bob and Flora Wilson.

This shows a combination of slip trailing, and sprigged on Wedgwood decoration, enhanced by enameled grapes and grape leaves. Basket 9" H. Vase, stand up handles 7" H. Collection of Bob and Flora Wilson.

Lavender colored Nippon Wedgwood items are scarce.

Following pages:
Lavender Wedgwood with orchids vase 9" H. Collection of Bob and Flora Wilson.

Lavender, classic Wedgwood design, Vase 7" H. Collection of Bob and Flora Wilson.

Lavender Wedgwood with orchids rose bowl 5½" H. Rare. Collection of Bob and Flora Wilson.

Lavender Wedgwood oval, open handled dish. Collection of Bob and Flora Wilson.

Reversed Wedgwood, and classic Wedgwood vases with figural Griffin bases. 8¼" H. Rare. Collection of Bob and Flora Wilson.

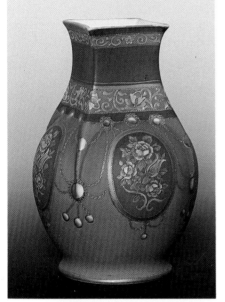

This shows a tan and cream colored Wedgwood, and classic Wedgwood design on scenic 11" H. vase. Notice that the scene in the vase on the left goes all the way to the base of the vase, and that in the vase on the right the scene stops and an additional band of Wedgwood decoration applied. The vases are both the same blank, decorated by different artists, each expressing himself in the differences of the finished product. Collection of Bob and Flora Wilson.

Very Rare coral colored Wedgwood 8¼" H. Vase. Collection of Lewis Longest Jr., FP, CPP.

Rare green Wedgwood tea set. Collection of Bob and Floral Wilson.

Chapter Twelve
Tapestry

In an effort to imitate the Royal Bayreuth rose tapestry technique, Japanese companies produced two different tapestry techniques of their own, "linen tapestry" and "sponge tapestry."

The linen technique involved applying a wet linen material to the surface of a pre-cast mold. The object was then bisque fired, at which time the material was consumed, leaving the texture similar to needlepoint tapestry. A scene was subsequently hand painted on the object. On some objects, a smooth linen was used in this process, while on others a more coarsely woven cloth which gives a rougher, heavier appearance.

The following Tapestry items are all marked with the "blue maple leaf" mark.

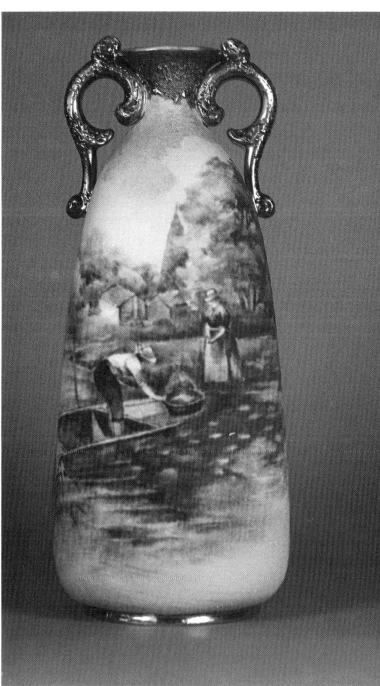

Linen all over tapestry vase "Man In a Boat" scene 8¼" H. Collection of Bob and Flora Wilson.

Linen all over tapestry bottle vase 8 ¼" H. Dorland/Pegg collection.

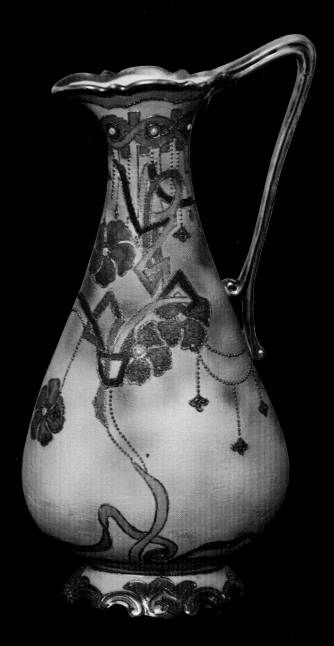

Linen all over tapestry ewer 10 ¾" H. Collection of Lewis Longest Jr., FP, CPP.

Linen tapestry "Castle Scene" center bands of Tapestry, with top and bottom bands of gold over-lay, gold beading and jewels. Top row vases 7 ¼" H. Bottom left to right vase 7 ¼" H. Pigtail handles, center vase 8" H. Stand up handles, ewer 7" H. Collections of Jess Berry and Gary Graves.

Linen tapestry, center tapestry band decorated with enameled Moriage flowers. Vase 8¼" H. Collection of Pat Goan.

Sponge tapestry. Vase 8¼" H. Decorated with heavy gold overlay designs. Collection of Harold and Audrey Eklund.

Linen tapestry, center band with top and bottom bands of floral. Vase 7" H. Pigtail handles. Collection of Bartley and Catherine Casteel.

Sponge tapestry. Vase 8½" H. Decorated with heavy gold overlay designs. Collection of Bob and Floral Wilson.

Sponge tapestry. Vase 7" H. Decorated with flowers. Collection of Phil and Jeanne Ferneks.

The linen fabric was applied with various methods to produce different results. Some objects were covered entirely with the linen, while other pieces had only the center section covered, leaving top and bottom bands free for decoration with heavy gold over-lay design, gold beading and multi-colored jewels. Another method was to apply only a front and back center medallion with tapestry and hand painted decorations of flowers, gold over-lay designs or heavy Moriage.

The sponge method technique is used almost exclusively on center medallions. In this method, the rough and uneven texture is coupled with small individual dots throughout. These dots look as though a sponge was dabbed onto the wet mold.

Since the majority of Nippon Tapestry items have the "Blue Maple leaf" mark, we assume that production was between 1891 and 1911. It is possible that between 1905 and 1911, tapestry pieces were made in small quantities, not mass-produced, thus making them rather more scarce and valuable.

Sponge tapestry bottle. Vase 7" H. Collection of Ralph and Cheryl DeWitt.

Chapter Thirteen
Cobalt

Nippon items decorated with cobalt blue under glaze possess superior quality art work and porcelain.

Until late in the nineteenth century, cobalt blue was found in Japan in a pebble which contains a mixture of cobalt, manganese, and iron. This source was hard to find, expensive, and difficult to apply. In the late 1860s, oxidized cobalt was imported to Japan. The imported cobalt oxide was more reliable (without shade variance), cheaper, and stronger, but much harsher and more brilliant in color. Cobalt oxide is the most powerful coloring oxide for tinting.

The intense dark cobalt blue items are often heavily decorated with gold overlay designs and heavy gold beading surrounding a center focal point of flowers, scenics, animals and birds. This combination of rich cobalt blue and heavy gold attracts a lot of attention.

Most Nippon cobalt items which bear the maple leaf mark or the M-in-wreath mark appear to be of higher quality porcelain and have much finer art work and color application. Pieces are found with the "crown," "pagoda," "R.C." and "rising sun" marks.

Cobalt and scenic pair of bolted urns 18½" H. Maple leaf mark. Collection of George and Donna Avezzano.

Cobalt and scenic bolted urn 24½" H. Maple leaf mark. Very rare. Collection of George and Donna Avezzano.

Cobalt and scenic footed chocolate pot 12½" H. Maple leaf mark.

Cobalt with white doves after dinner demi-tea set. Collection of Ralph and Cheryl DeWitt.

Cobalt and mountain scene pitcher 9½" H. Maple leaf mark.

Cobalt and swans bolted urn 14½" H. Maple leaf mark. Collection of George and Donna Avezzano.

Cobalt and swans vase, loop handles 7½" H. Maple leaf mark.
Collection Rolfes & Virginia Hensley.

Cobalt and scenic deer on a hill plate 10" W. Man on a camel Plate
10" W. Maple leaf mark.

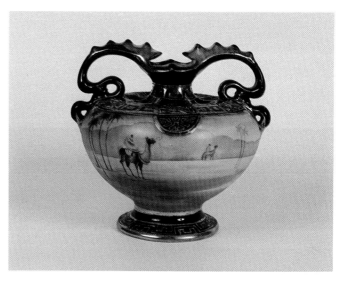

Cobalt and man on a camel vase 10½" H. Maple leaf mark.

Cobalt and swans covered urn 13¾" H. Maple leaf mark. Collection
of Harold and Audrey Eklund.

Cobalt and roses unusual dish 10½" H. x 10¼" W. Maple leaf
mark. Collection of Harold and Audrey Eklund.

Cobalt and ostrich vase 14" H.
Front view, M-in-wreath mark.
Collection of Phil and Jeanne
Fernkes.

Back view.

Cobalt and gold overlay, with white
enameled flowers 10½" H. Imperial
Nippon mark. Collecions of Jess Berry
and Gary Graves.

Cobalt and ostrich's pair of vases 9¼" H. Plaque 10" W. Black
border. M-in-wreath mark.

Cobalt and gold overlay pierced handled cake plate 10½". Maple leaf mark. Collection of Lewis Longest Jr., FP, CPP.

Cobalt and gold overlay vase 15¾" H. Vase 12½" H. x 24½" W. Maple leaf mark. Collection of George and Donna Avezzano.

Cobalt and roses covered urn 16". Unmarked.

Planter outside and inside liner. Collection of Lewis Longest Jr., FP, CPP.

Cobalt and gold planter 3 3/8″ H. Two pieces. Cheery blossom Nippon mark.

Cobalt and violets basket 6″ H. x 5″ W. Dowsie Nippon mark. Collection of Lewis Longest Jr., FP, CPP.

Cobalt gold and white chocolate set with 4 cups and saucers. Maple leaf mark. Collection of Howard and Shirley Grubka.

Chapter Fourteen
Lamps

There are very few Nippon lamps originally made to be wired for electricity, but they can be identified by the Nippon mark in it's entirety off to the side of a glazed hole. The more usual Nippon lamps began as a vase which was drilled in order to make it into a lamp; the drilled hole on these can be directly through the Nippon backstamp and the hole is un-glazed.

Candlelamps consist of a candlestick with a porcelain shade which is the same decoration as the porcelain base. Electric candle lamps are not known to exist. 14" H. M-in-wreath mark. Collection of Harold and Audrey Eklund. 15" H. M-in-wreath mark. Collection of Cathy Keys. Very Rare.

Nippon electric night lights can be found in the shape of rabbits, owls, and a very rare dutch girl lamp. The rabbit night light lifts off its base revealing factory drilled holes guiding the electric cord and a depression in the porcelain to accommodate the bulb. Lamp 6¼" H. M-in-wreath mark. Dorland/Pegg collection. Very Rare. Owl night light. M-in-wreath mark. Collection of Roger Zeefe. Very Rare.

Original lamp, Nippon mark can be seen in it's entirety off to one side. Bolted two piece. Blue Maple leaf mark. 15¾" H.

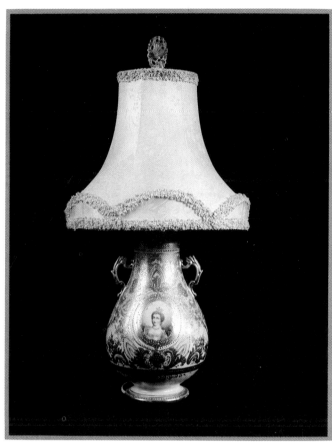

Queen Victoria portrait lamp 10½" H. Over all height 23½". Green Maple leaf mark.

An original boudoir lamp has a glazed hole to hold the pull chain for turning the lamp on and off, a cord guide and notches, which serve as locks to secure the porcelain globe. Very, very rare. As of this publication the only one known in existence. M-in-wreath mark. Collection of Rita and Bob Gillis.

Pair of Portrait Queen Louise lamps 19" H. Blue Maple leaf mark. Collections of Jess Berry and Gary Graves.

I suspect that the lamps below are vases which have been turned into lamps. The only way to know for sure would to take them apart from the base and check to see the mark is off to one side or the whole is drilled thru the mark.

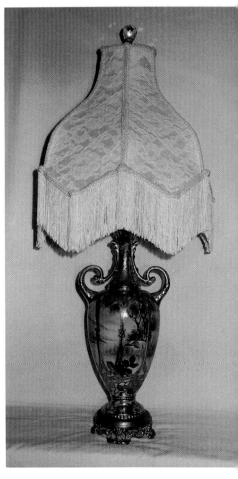

Lamp 15" H. Over all height 32". Collection of Ted and Nita Ensign.

Lamp 10½" H.

Lamp 11" H. Collection of Wayne and Barbara Bryant.

Vase converted to lamp 10" H. Collection of Cathy Keys.

Chapter Fifteen
Molded-In-Relief, about 1911-1921

Molded Nippon items have a three dimensional appearance ranging from high, medium, and low relief. High relief is significantly raised whereas low relief is only slightly raised.

These exotic and theatrical items were produced by the Noritake Company after 1911 until approximately 1921. Their different, more western style indicates that they were created not by a Japanese designer, but rather a United States buyer who ordered the production through the Morimura Brothers in Japan. The majority of these items bear the M-in-wreath mark.

In these goods, the raised surface is part of the original mold. An artist incised a design into the mold, removed parts of the mold, created a concave area into which the liquid clay was poured, thus filling in the cut-out design. These items all appear to have had some type of upward pressure from the underside.

This Egyptian God humidor clearly illustrates the portions which protrude over the base. Look closely at the lid where you will find a scarab which is a large beetle held sacred by the ancient Egyptians.

Relief designs, which typically appeal to masculine collectors, feature animals, birds, humans and occasionally landscapes. They can be found on ashtrays, ferners, humidors, plaques, vases and tankard sets. With the exception of humidors, these items seem to be designed for decorative rather than functional purposes. Humidors were designed to house and keep fresh tobacco products and because of their utilitarian nature, little or no care was taken to ensure longevity of the lids. Therefore, humidors with original lids are among the rarest of the molded-in-relief items.

It is an obvious truism that the Japanese artists had great difficulty painting a typically American-looking face as you can see when you take a good look at some of the Indian items, which show Indians looking somewhat like a cross between Japanese and Westerners. Apparently, artists had no first hand knowledge about an Indians' appearance. Some plaques depict Indians' riding horseback with palm trees in the background further indicating how little the Japanese understood western life.

Fisherman rectangular plaque 10½" W. x 13" H. Very rare. Collection of Joan Van Patten.

Fisherman vase 8½" H. Very very Rare. Dorland/Pegg collection.

Fisherman wine jug. Rare. Collection of Joan Van Patten.

Fisherman tankard set tankard 11½" H. Mugs 4¾" H. Very rare. Collection of Joan Van Patten.

Fisherman humidor 7½" H. Very rare. Collection of Joan Van Patten.

Blond slave or Lady Godiva rectangular plaque 14" W. Very rare.
Dorland/Pegg collection.

Bedouins on horseback. Rare. Collection of Roger Zeefe.

Bedouin along side horse. 10" H. Rare. Dorland/Pegg collection.

Children under the tree. 12½" H. Very rare. Collection of Roger Zeefe.

Children under the tree humidor 6¾" H. The vase and humidor are the only known Children under the tree items known to exist. The color on these two items is different from the color on most molded-in-relief items, in the sense that the colors are more vibrant and there is lots of color contrast. Very very rare. Collection of Roger Zeefe.

Johnny Appleseed or The Sower. Vase 10½" H. Plaque 12" W. Scarce. Johnny Appleseed was the nickname of John Chapman (1774-1845), a New England eccentric who settled (about 1800 or 1810) in the Ohio valley and made it his business to plant apple seeds all over the countryside and to tend the growing trees. He became the hero of a body of popular legends of great folkloristic interest. The United States version Johnny Appleseed, the same scene is well known by the french as "Le Femeur" which translates into English as "The Sower," this is another example of a copy of the 1850 Millet oil panting known as the "Sower." Dorland/Pegg collection.

Apollo and rearing dogs. Vase 9½" H. Humidor 6½" H. Plaque 12" W. Rare. Dorland/Pegg collection.

Indian and bear humidor 7" H. Showing front, side and back view of molded-in-relief wrap around decoration. Very rare. Collection of Roger Zeefe.

Twin Indian profile three color variations, with the rarest being the Wedgwood version. The young men of Indian societies were either warriors or hunters. Each class had its own leader. This cameo type molded-in-relief plaque is a tribute paid to those leaders, it features the warrior in full feather bonnet and the hunter clad in his buffalo cap, complete with horns. These were important men, since it was their responsibility to provide protection and food for their tribe. Dorland/Pegg collection.

Indian ashtray 6½" L. Very rare. The Indians, found on Nippon pieces commemorate their way of life, their rituals and three renowned chiefs who led their tribes in the Great Indian Wars.

The chiefs of the Northeastern tribes wore feathered bonnets made of feathers shorter in length than those of the Plains tribes. They wore this headdress only when riding a horse. This ashtray shows the headdress in bright colored feathers and is framed with Indian designs. Dorland/Pegg collection.

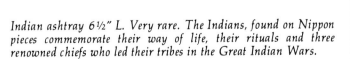

Humidor 7¼" H. Very rare. This Indian-head humidor is perhaps the most dramatic tribute to Indian spiritual life. Every tribe has its spiritual leader or Medicine Man and it was left to him to provide the answers to both health and strategy.

One of the rituals used to obtain answers is told in detail in this Nippon humidor. The knob on the cover is in the shape of the Lotus flower, often dried and smoked before consulting the Gods. The eyes of the Indian are blackened with soot to block out evil spirits. Adorned in proper head dress, beads and robes to consult the Gods, he prayed in the direction of the sun, wind and rain (thus the three heads). The resulting visions (know to us as hallucinations) provided answers to the perplexities that faced him.

Without a doubt, this Nippon humidor holds the same outstanding position in Nippon collecting as did the Indian it commemorates. Collection of Roger Zeefe.

Fire in the forest humidor 7" H. The Indians were notorious horse thieves. It was not unusual for them to burn out both white settlers and the camps of neighboring tribes when on a horse stealing raid. This humidor with its flaming orange and black fire background shows an Indian leading a frightened horse. Dorland/Pegg collection.

Indian on horse back charger 15" W. and plaque 10½" W. Here we see our Indian warriors charging forth into battle with guns rather than bows and arrows. As the Great Indian Wars progressed, the Indians acquired guns. Sometimes stolen or taken from dead soldiers, but most often bought with gems and furs from profiteering white men. Dorland/Pegg collection.

Cigar ashtray with Molded-in-relief Indian head. Rare. Collection of Roger Zeefe.

Indian head bookends 5 ⅞" W. x 5 ¾" H. Very very rare. Collection of Harold and Audrey Eklund.

Indian hunting buffalo plaque 10½" W. Very very rare, only one known to exist. Collection of Lee and Donna Call.

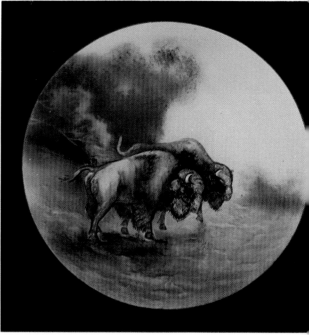

Buffalo plaque 10½" W. Dorland/Pegg collection.

Horse head plaque 10½" W. Scarce. This also comes in black. Dorland/Pegg collection.

Horse with horseshoe humidor 8" H. Scarce. Collection of Roger Zeefe.

Three pony plaque 10½" W. Humidor 7½" H. Rare. Collection of Roger Zeefe.

Three horse head humidor showing color variations 7" H. Collection of Bob and Flora Wilson.

Camel and rider 7½" H. Scarce. Collection of Roger Zeefe.

Beggar man vase 10" H. This vase comes in three different color variations yellow, gray, and blue. Scarce. Dorland/Pegg collection.

Camel and rider plaque 10½" W. Scarce. Collection of Roger Zeefe.

Camel kneeling humidors in two color variations 6½" H. Very rare. Collection of Roger Zeefe.

Stag tankard set tankard ll½" H,
mugs 5" H. This set also come in a
very rare yellow. Dorland/Pegg
collection.

Full face lion plaque's 10½" W.
Two color variations. Scarce.
Dorland/Pegg collection.

Lion and lioness plaque 10½" W. Dorland/Pegg collection

Lion and Lioness humidor 7¼" H. Collection of Roger Zeefe.

Lion and python ferner 8½" W. x 5¼" H. Humidor 6¾" H. Dorland/Pegg collection.

Figural tiger ashtray 6¼" W. Rare. Dorland/Pegg collection.

Tiger humidor 7¼" H. Rare. Dorland/Pegg collection.

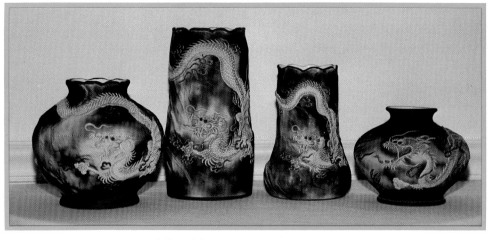

Jeweled eyed dragon vase 6½" H., 10½" H., 7½" H. Last vase is tapestry rather than molded-in-relief. Scarce. Collection of Wayne and Mary Myers.

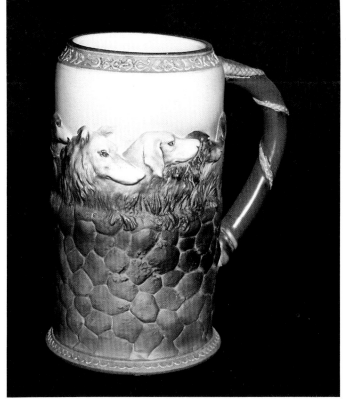

Dog stein with leash handle 7" H. Collection of Roger Zeefe.

Terrier humidor. 7½" H. Collection of Roger Zeefe.

Three dog plaque 10½" W. Rare. Collection of Roger Zeefe.

Collie humidor 6¼" H. Collection of Roger Zeefe.

Dogs ashtray 7" W. Scarce. Collection of Roger Zeefe

Collie and Terrier charger 15½" W. Plaque 10½" W. Dorland/Pegg collection.

Bulldog plaque's 10½" W. Two color variations. Dorland/Pegg collection.

Figural great dane ashtray with marbleized background. Collection of Roger Zeefe.

Dog ashtray 5¾" W. Collection of Roger Zeefe.

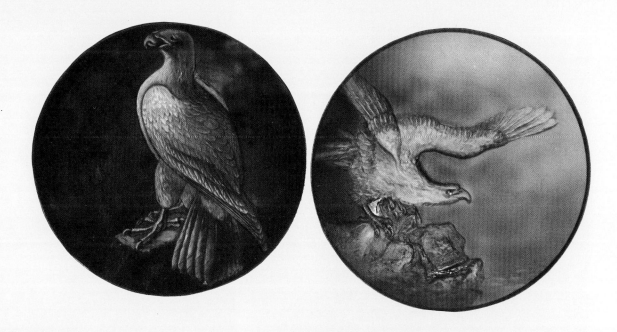

One color variation of sitting eagle and flying eagle. Very rare. Dorland/Pegg collection.

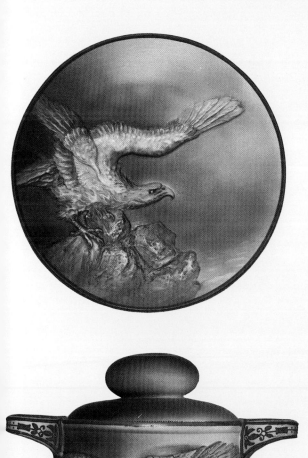

Colorful version of sitting eagle 10½" W. Very rare. Collection of Roger Zeefe.

Flying eagle humidor 7½" H. Plaque 10½" W., same color decoration. Very Rare. Collection of Roger Zeefe.

Owl in a treestump humidor 7" H. Scarce. Collection of Roger Zeefe.

Owls on a branch 10" H. vase. Scarce. Dorland/Pegg collection.

Owls on a branch stein 7" H. Very rare. Collection of Roger Zeefe.

Figural owl vase 9" H. Scarce. Dorland/Pegg collection.

Figural owls ferner 5″ W. Dorland/Pegg collection.

Owl humidor 7″ H. Collection of Roger Zeefe.

Figural Penguins ashtray 5″ H. x 6″ W. Scarce.
Dorland/Pegg collection.

Figural seal ashtray 3½″ H. x 7″ W. Scarce.
Dorland/Pegg collection.

Swan vase 8″ H. Rare. Dorland/Pegg collection.

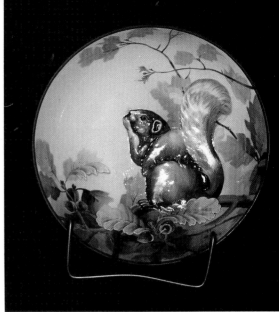

Figural squirrel bowl 10" W. Dorland/Pegg collection.

Squirrel eating an acorn in shiny finish bowl 10" W. Dorland/Pegg collection.

Monks humidor front and back view 7½" H. Rare. Collection of Roger Zeefe.

Egyptian warriors, mythological birds with twisted rope edging 5½"
H. x 4¼" W. Very rare. Collection of Harold and Audrey Eklund.

Elephant footed vase 8" H. Dorland/Pegg collection.

Elephant ferner 4½" H. x 5" W. Dorland/Pegg collection.

Ferner with rams head columns. Scarce. Dorland/Pegg collection.

Village vase 5½" H. Dorland/Pegg collection.

Mountain side flower plaque 10¼" W. Vase 8" H. Very rare. Collection of Roger Zeefe.

Chapter Sixteen
Indians

All of the following Indian items are marked with the M-in-wreath mark.

Plaque 10" W. Rare. Dorland/Pegg collection.

Indian and goose bolted urn 24½" H. Very Rare. Collection of Rita and Bob Gillis.

Indian plaque 11" W. Rare. Dorland/Pegg collection.

Stein 7" H. Rare. Collection of Rita and Bob Gillis.

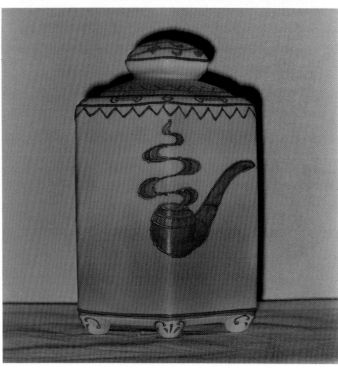

Six-sided Humidor on bull feet, 6¾" H. Front side shows Indian in full headdress, back shows smoking pipe. Rare. The decoration on this and the following items was achieved by a Moriage applied technique that has the design incised into it. Collection of Jerry and Linda Cox.

Plaque 10" W. Rare. Collection of Bob and Floral Wilson.

Chief Sitting Bull plaque 10" W. Heavy Moriage trim. Rare. Collection of Rita and Bob Gillis.

Close up of Chief Sitting Bull who was the leader of the Hunkpapa Sioux tribe that roamed the plains of Iowa. He came to be known as the greatest of Indian statesmen, a spiritual leader and a very great human being. He led his tribe in wars, instigated spiritual dances know as Indian Ghost Dances and toured the United States with Buffalo Bill Cody's Wild West Show. In December 1890 he died of gunshot wounds during a misunderstanding with some soldiers.

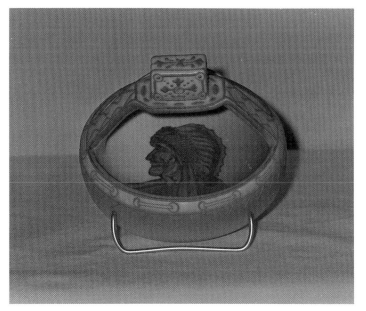

Ashtray with attached match box holder. 3½" H. x 4¾" W. Rare. Collection of Jerry and Linda Cox.

Nappy 5" W. Scarce. Collection of Bartley and Catherine Casteel.

Chief Sitting Bull Humidor, 6½" x 5". W. Karg Collection of Khurana Doll Outlet.

Chief Joseph Humidor, 6" x 3½". Chief Joseph, an Indian of the Nez Perce Indian tribe, of Northern Oregon, was a peaceful man by nature. He earned respect for his well organized, defensive battles against United States forces and was considered the greatest of all Indian Generals. He was later captured 30 miles from the Canadian border and sent to Colville reservation in Washington. Here he lived out his remaining days depressed over the neglect of his tribe. He died of a "Broken Heart" in late 1904. Collection of Joe Galler.

Chapter Seventeen
Steins—Mugs

Steins are 7" H. and all marked with the Maple leaf mark or the M-in-wreath mark. Collection of Roger Zeefe.

"Hunt Scene" stein.

Moriage decorated stein.

"Galle Scene" stein.

"English Cottage Scene" stein.

Enameled steins.

"Windmill Scene."

Arabs at the Wall.

Scenic steins.

Mugs are all 5½ H. and all marked with the M-in-wreath mark.

Arab by the campfire.

Chapter Eighteen
Jugs

Wine jug 11" H. M-in-wreath mark. Original wicker basket. Collection of Phil and Jeanne Fernkes.

Wine jug 9½" H. "Dutch Moonlit scene." M-in-wreath mark. Private collection.

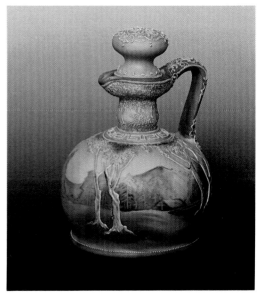

Moriage "White Woodland Scene" whiskey jug. Maple leaf mark. Collection of Lewis Longest Jr., FP, CPP.

Moriage wine jug, 8½" H. Moriage frogs beating each other up with stick. Scarce. Collection of Jerry and Linda Cox.

Wine jug 6½" H. Maple leaf mark. Missing the stopper. Collection of Lewis Longest Jr., FP, CPP.

Wine jug 8" H. M-in-wreath mark. Collections of Jess Berry and Gary Graves.

Moriage wine jug. 8¼" H. Maple leaf mark. Collection of Allan and Beverly Shaw.

Moriage wine jug 7¼" H. Maple leaf mark. Collection of Jerry and Linda Cox.

Chapter Nineteen
Humidor—Smoke Items

When cigars, pipe smoking and rolling your own cigarettes were fashionable, humidors were used to keep cigars and loose tobacco moist. A humidor lid has a receptacle for a damp sponge or piece of fresh apple which provided moisture. Most Nippon humidors bear the M-in-wreath mark.

7½" H. M-in-wreath mark. Painted birds with moriage trim. Collection of Rita and Bob Gillis.

8" H. Painted trailing wisteria and moriage trailing wisteria. Collection of Lewis Longest, Jr., FP, CPP.

7½" H. M-in-wreath mark. Collection of Rita and Bob Gillis.

5" H. Blue Maple leaf mark. Collection of Rolfes and Virginia Hensley.

7¼" H. M-in-wreath mark. Collection of Rita and Bob Gillis.

6½" H. M-in-wreath mark. Three handled "Dutch Moonlit scene." Private collection.

7½" H. "Dutchman and the Cat." M-in-wreath mark. Collection of Rita and Bob Gillis.

6¼" H. M-in-wreath mark. Collection of Rita and Bob Gillis.

3½" H. M-in-wreath mark. Egyptian scene. Collection of Dr. and Mrs. Jody Ginsberg.

5" H. "Nile scene" Blue Maple leaf mark. Collection of Bartley and Catherine Casteel.

7 1/2" H. M-in-wreath mark. Enameled trees and decoration.
Collection of Rita and Bob Gillis.

6 1/4" H. M-in-wreath mark.
Collection of Cathy Keys.

Ashtray 5 1/2" W. M-in-wreath
mark. Collection of Bartley and
Catherine Casteel.

7 1/2" H. Collection of Rita and Bob Gillis.

Left to right: 7" Hand-painted Nippon mark, 5¾" H. Maple leaf mark. 4½" H. Imperial Nippon mark. 5¾" H. Maple leaf mark. Collection of Lewis Longest Jr., FP, CPP.

Cigarette boxes, 4½" W. M-in-wreath mark. Collection of Rita and Bob Gillis.

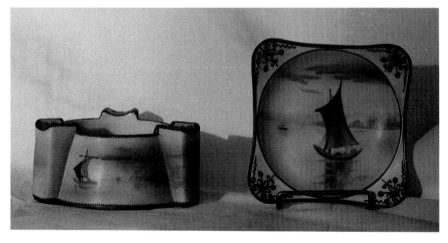

Ashtray 5¼" W. Nappy 4¾" W. M-in-wreath mark. Collection of Bartley and Catherine Casteel.

Combination ashtray and match box holder, this one is unique in that the match box holder is removable from the ashtray. Scarce. Collection of Polly Frye.

Combination ashtray and match box holder. 3½" H. x 4" W. Collection of George and Doris Myers.

Combination ashtray and match box holder. M-in-wreath mark. Collection of Bartley and Catherine Casteel.

Miniature loving cup 3¾" H. Match box holder 2¾" H. M-in-wreath mark, Scarce. Collection of Bob and Flora Wilson.

Ashtray 4¼" W. M-in-wreath mark. Collection of Dr. and Mrs. Jody Ginsberg.

Smoke set, tray 9¾" W. Match holder 3" H. x 4" W., Humidor 5¾" H. x 3½" W. Ashtray 3¼" W. M-in-wreath mark. Rare. Collection of George and Doris Myers.

Chapter Twenty
Desk Sets

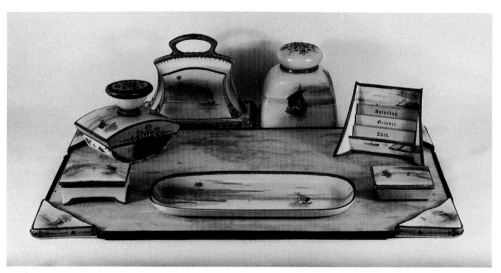

Complete desk set. Standing envelope holder, inkwell, rocking blotter with original brass roller, standing calendar holder with original paper month and days calendar, footed double stamp box, pen tray, single stamp box, original blotter with four blotter corners. M-in-wreath mark. Very Rare. Harold and Audrey Eklund collection.

Inkwell with pen rest, 3½" H. x 4½" W. RC hand-painted Nippon mark. Paper label attached which reads "Compliments of the Morimura Brothers, 1914." Collection of Rolfes and Virginia Hensley.

Rocking blotter, original brass roller, 4½" W. M-in-wreath mark. Collection of Cathy Keys.

Desk set. Standing calendar, 3" H. x 4" W. Inkwell, 4" H. Stamp box 1½" H. x 2¾" W. Four blotter corners. RC hand-painted Nippon mark. Scarce. Collection of Bartley and Catherine Casteel.

Chapter Twentyone
Chocolate, Tea Sets

There are various opinions on what comprises a "complete" chocolate or tea set. These views range from the pot with two, four, or six matching cups and saucers. We know that the Japanese people of the Nippon era preferred sets which included odd numbers of cups and saucers: particularly popular were sets of three, five, and seven. Not until World War I were there sets which included six cups and saucers.

By scanning old catalogs one finds that many of the chocolate and tea pots were offered for sale singularly. One could order a pot, and as many cups and saucers as one needed. Each set ordered could contain a different number of cups and saucers. This number often depends upon how much space a collector has to display one or more sets.

Nippon was produced as chocolate sets, tea sets, after dinner coffee sets, demitasse after dinner sets, and lemonade sets. The position of the spout determines the type of set each pot belongs to.

A chocolate pot spout comes directly from the top of the 8" to 13" tall pot. The cups are tall and narrow.

The lemonade pitcher spout also comes directly from the top of the pitcher, but the lemonade pitcher is quite fat and does not require a lid. Lemonade cups are taller than chocolate cups and have no saucers.

The spout of a tea pot begins at the base of a 4"H. to 6½"H pot and extends out in a fat curved manor. Tea set cups are low and round.

An after-dinner coffee pot spout begins mid-section on the pot and is long and slender. The demitasse after dinner coffee pots are similar to the after dinner pots, but smaller.

Footed Chocolate pot 10¼" H. Maple leaf mark. Collection of Lewis Longest, Jr., FP, CPP.

Chocolate set, two cups and saucers. Pot, 9½" H. M-in wreath mark. Ralph and Cheryl DeWitt.

Chocolate set, four cups and saucers. Pot, 9¼" H. M-in-wreath mark.

Chocolate set, two cups and saucers. Pot, 9" H. Collection of Wayne and Barbara Bryant.

Chocolate set, four cups and saucers. Pot, 8". M-in-wreath mark. Horton collection.

Chocolate set, four cups and saucers. Howard and Shirley Grubka collection.

Chocolate set, four cups and saucers. Pot, 9" H. M-in-wreath mark. Howard and Shirley Grubka.

Chocolate pot, 9½" H. Maple leaf mark.

Chocolate set, R.S. Prussia mold, five cups and saucers. Pot, 11" H. Maple leaf mark.

A Chocolate set, five cups and saucers. Pot, 9" H. This set has various scenes of San Francisco, California. The six scenes on the pot are the Phelan building, Seals on seal rocks, Cliff house, Pacific and Commercial Building, and Emporium. Cup scenes are Union Terry Depot, The new cliff house, Stone Lake on Strawberry Hill (Golden Gate Park), Mission Delores. At the concert (Golden Gate Park). Rare. Collection of Harold and Audrey Eklund.

Chocolate set, four cups and saucers. Pot, 9½" H.

Close up of artist's signature found on pot and cups. This signature indicates that this set was sent to the United States as a blank and decorated at one of the china painting studios. Collection of Lewis Longest, Jr., CPP.

Chocolate set, four cups and saucers. Pot, 10" H. M-in-wreath mark. Ralph and Cheryl DeWitt collection.

Chocolate set, four cups and saucers. Howard and Shirley Grubka collection.

Chocolate set, five cups and saucers. Pot, 10½" H. Collection of Lewis Longest Jr., FP, CPP.

Chocolate set, six cups and saucers. Pot, 9" H. M-in-wreath mark. Collection of Rolfes and Virginia Hensley.

Chocolate set, six cups and saucers. Heavily jeweled, R. S. Prussia shape. Pot, 10½" H. M-in-wreath mark. Scarce.

Chocolate set, six cups and saucers. Pot, ll" H. Maple leaf mark. Scarce.

Egyptian chocolate set, six cups and saucers. Norm and Fran Miller collection.

Chocolate set, six cups and saucers. Pot, 9" H. M-in-wreath mark. Collection of Wayland and Brenda Horton.

Tea pot spouts start at the bottom of the pot and are long and narrow.

Tea pot, pedestal base. 6" H. Collection of Dr. and Mrs. Jody Ginsberg.

Tea set. Pot, cream pitcher, sugar bowl, five cups and saucers, footed. Collection of Ted and Nita Ensign.

Tea set. Pot, cream pitcher, sugar bowl, four cups and saucers, footed. Ralph and Cheryl DeWitt collection.

Tea pot, cream pitcher and sugar bowl, footed, R. S. Prussia shape, Maple leaf mark.

Coffee pot spouts start at the mid-section of the pot and are long and narrow.

After dinner demitasse coffee set. Tray, 13" L., Tea pot, 6¼" H., Cream pitcher, sugar bowl and four cups and saucers. M-in-wreath mark. Collection of Rolfes and Virginia Hensley.

Lemonade set.

Lemonade set.

Chapter Twentytwo
Dresser Items

Perfume bottle, 5¾" H. Maple leaf mark. Collection of Wayne and Barbara Bryant.

Perfume bottle with moriage trim, 3¼" H. M-in-wreath mark. Collection of Jerry and Linda Cox.

Dresser set candlesticks, 6" H. Large covered jar 3¾" H. Small covered jar, 2¾" H. Ring tree, 2½" H. Pin tray, 5" W. L & C Nippon mark. Collection of Dr. and Mrs. Jody Ginsberg.

Dresser set. Tray 11" W. X 8" H. Heart-shaped powder box, hair receiver, and pin tray, 4½" W. X 5" H. Maple leaf mark. Collection of Bartley and Catherine Casteel.

Manicure set. Tray, 7" W. Tall covered jar, 2¼" H., Medium covered jar, 1¾" H. Small covered jar, 1¼" H. M-in-wreath mark. Collection of George and Doris Myers.

Perfume bottle, 4½" H. Covered box, 3" H. X 4" W. Dutch shoe 3½" W. M-in-wreath mark. Collection of Bartley and Catherine Casteel.

Dresser set. Tray 11½" W. Footed powder box, hair receiver, open hat pin holder, ring tree, and pin tray. M-in-wreath mark. Cathy Keyes collection.

Perfume bottle 4¼" H. M-in-wreath mark. Collection of Cathy Keys.

Lady's spittoon, 2" H. X 3 1/8" W. unmarked, scarce. Perfume bottle, 5" H. RC mark. Ring tree, 2 1/4" H. X 3 1/2" W. Private collection.

Closed hat pin holder. Maple leaf mark. Polly Frye collection.

Stick pin holder. Maple leaf mark. Scarce. Private collection.

Open hat pin holder. M-in-wreath mark. Collection of George and Doris Myers.

Large "Ruins scene" powder box, 8" W. M-in-wreath mark. Collections of Jess Berry and Gary Graves.

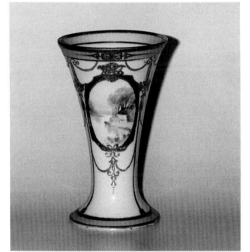

Tooth brush holder, 5½" H. M-in-wreath mark. Collection of Wayne and Barbara Bryant.

Large powder box, 7" W. M-in-wreath mark.

Open hat pin holder, 4¾" H. M-in-wreath mark. Closed hat pin holder, 4½" H. Cherry blossom mark. Open hat pin holder, 4¾" H. Rising Sun mark. Collection of Dr. and Mrs. Jody Ginsberg.

Covered boxes.

Pedestal-base covered trinkets, Maple leaf mark.

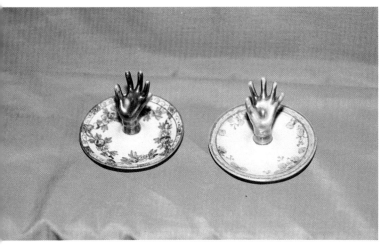

Ring trees, M-in-wreath mark. Olin and Grace Harkleroad collection.

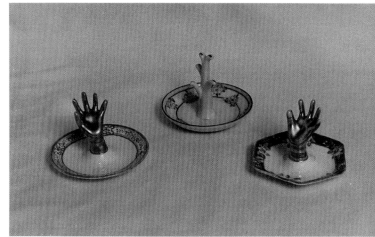

Ring trees, 2¼″ H. M-in-wreath mark. 2½″ H. Cherry blossom mark. 2¼″ H. M-in-wreath mark. Collection of Dr. and Mrs. Jody Ginsberg.

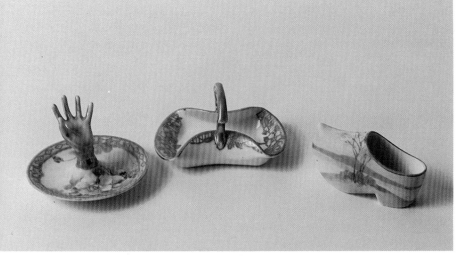

Ring tree, Miniature basket, and Dutch shoe, M-in-wreath mark.

Hair pin holders, 3¼″ H. M-in-wreath mark, scarce.

Chapter Twentythree
Dolls: 1914-1921

At the outbreak of World War I, in 1914, German doll makers converted doll factories to war time activities, creating a void of new bisque doll heads and bodies. As a leading Japanese importing house, The Morimura Brothers promptly recognized this as opportunity for them. Experts were sent to Japan with instructions to build a factory for the manufacture of dolls.

One of the most difficult problems was the modeling of European expression. Even with the original model before him, the Japanese artisans worked persistently to achieve a perfect reproduction. Some are excellent, high quality dolls. The later the doll, the better the quality. The porcelain bisque heads were made in Kyoto and the bodies in Osaka. Also, a few German head and body molds were brought into Japan. Glass eyes had to be made. The proper elastic to connect the joints had to be secured; and the proper material to make the body durable had to be found.

"In spite of all the care that was taken, the first product did not turn out well, and heavy losses were entailed by those backing the enterprise. All the wise-acres joined in the chorus "We told you so", "It can't be done" etc. The Japanese, however, refused to be discouraged. They went at the problem with renewed vigor. Profiting by past experience, the first mistakes were eliminated and success rewarded their persistent efforts. At last a doll was produced which has attracted considerable attention."(The Collector's Encyclopedia of Dolls, Coleman).

Ever since the advent of the doll line, the entire factory output was sold the year previous to delivery date.

In July of 1917, Frederick Langfelder of New York City, a United States citizen, applied for a United States design patent for a doll with eyes looking to the side and dressed in a bathing suit. The Morimura Bros. firm was the assignee and the patent was granted in October, 1917, for a period of seven years.

Morimura Bros. also handled dolls made completely in America. In 1918, they took the entire year's production of the Bester Dolls Manufacturing Co. of Bloomfield, NJ. These "Bester Dolls" were fully ball-jointed in sizes 16. 18. 20. 22, 25. and 26 inches tall.

Immediately after the First World War, in December, 1918, PLAYTHINGS magazine carried a full page advertisement for Morimura Brothers. that stated: Japanese Dolls and Toys on import. // The Famous 'Baby Ella' Character Dolls // Bisque Head French Glass Moving Eyes with or without eyelashes. With or without

Doll, 23" H., bisque shoulder plate on jointed kid body with bisque lower arms, fixed brown eyes, open mouth with tongue and four teeth. Mark #D2. Damaske collection.

Half doll. Dorland/Pegg collection.

wigs (Mohair and Natural Hair), 16 to 57 centimeters. (6½" to 23") // JOINTED DOLLS 23 to 54 centimeters (9" to 21½") with or without eyelashes. Natural Hair Wigs. // 'KIDOLYN' Kid body Dolls. Hip Jointed, Jointed Arms. Hip and Knee Jointed.// BISQUE BABIES of all descriptions.// FULL LINE OF HEADS FOR JOINTED DOLLS. With or without wigs. With or without Eyelashes."

It appears the Morimuras had been able to obtain some glass eyes from France for their bisque heads. They advertised "French" glass eyes for several years. The "Kidolyn" body dolls were made with the NE PLUS ULTRA type of pin joint at the hips. The bisque babies were made with bent limbs and with wigs or so-called bald heads. In *Playthings*, September 1920, Mourima Brothers advertised "Baby Ella". 'Baby Rose', 'My Darling', 'First Prize Baby' // Bisque Dolls, full jointed, Kidaline Body, Baby Dolls. // Long curled wigs of natural hair, mohair wigs. // Dolls with bald heads. // China Limb Dolls, repeating our 1919 line. // Celluloid Dolls, Straight Limb and celluloid character babies in all sizes. // Our 'Dolly Doll' in the bathing suit."

These same dolls were advertised in 1920, plus My Sweetheart, Baby O'Mine, and Nankeen Dolls, (which were probably dolls with china heads and china limbs on nankeen [cotton] bodies). Morimura Brothers referred to their dolls as "M.B." dolls in 1921, which suggests that, these initials were widely recognized by the trade then. They continued to advertise bisque, celluloid, and china limb dolls as well as Kidaline body dolls in 1921.

German dolls had returned to the American market in quantity by 1922, and before January, 1922, Morimura Brothers Miscellaneous Import Department, which handled their dolls, was taken over by Langfelder, Homma & Hayward Inc. of New York City, which handled both Japanese and German dolls. Morimura Brothers continued as a Japanese Import House, but no record has been found of their handling dolls after 1922.

The Morimura all-bisque dolls labeled "Baby Darling" on stickers on the stomach may have been the "My Darling" dolls advertised in 1919 and 1920. "My Darling" was a trademark of Kammer & Reinhardt, a circumstance that may have been responsible for the alteration in name.

Doll, 23" H. Bisque socket head on excellent "signed" German ball-jointed composition body, brown sleep eyes, open mouth with four teeth, human hair wig. Mark #D10. Damaske collection.

Doll, 21" H. Bisque socket head on kidalene, straw filled body, bisque lower arms, blue sleep eyes, four teeth. Mark #D10. Damaske collection.

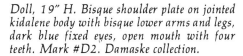

Doll, 19" H. Bisque shoulder plate on jointed kidalene body with bisque lower arms and legs, dark blue fixed eyes, open mouth with four teeth. Mark #D2. Damaske collection.

Doll 21" Tall. Bisque socket head on nice ball-jointed German composition body, light blue sleep eyes, open mouth with tongue and four teeth. Mark #D5. Damaske collection.

Doll, 21" H. Bisque socket head on ball-jointed composition body, brown sleep eyes, open mouth with four teeth. Mark #D11. Damaske collection.

Doll care: Storage and cleaning

The elements which cause the most damage to dolls are dust, heat, dampness, moths and light. To preserve your dolls:

1. Do not store dolls in attics or basements. A dry basement with controlled humidity and temperature may be all right. 2. Do not display dolls where they are in direct sunlight or even bright artificial light for any extended length of time. 3. Storing dolls in closed cabinets or "dolly dusters" avoids accumulated dust. 4. When storing dolls, especially composition dolls, never use a plastic bag. Instead, use non-acid tissue paper or an old sheet or pillow case. 5. For storage of cloth dolls (doll clothes and wigs) which attract moths, beetles and mice, a few moth balls placed within the folds of the wrappings but not touching the doll will keep the pests away. Also, Fels Naptha soap cut in small pieces and placed in a cabinet or drawer works well as a pest deterrent. 6. If the original box is included with your doll, and you have limited storage space, collapse the box down, but by all means do not throw it away. Original boxes are highly prized and add value to the doll for serious collectors. 7. Do not destroy "original" clothes which came with the doll, or were made by or for the original owner. Should you choose to re-dress the doll to better suit your taste, or if the clothes are stained or damaged, keep the original clothes, label them, and pass them along to the next owner. 8. When storing a bisque-head doll with glass eyes, or any separate eyes, store them face down; this helps to prevent the eyes from falling loose and perhaps breaking the eyes or the head.

When cleaning a small bisque doll or a bisque head doll, a good soap and water cleansing usually does quite well. More serious dirt marks can be removed with a very mild abrasive such as "Softscrub," "409," or "Fantastic" and gentle buffing. Mild soap on a damp cloth will clean most leather or composition bodies. Never put water directly on composition bodies. Most bisque-head dolls have human hair or mohair wigs. A human hair wig can be gently washed with a baby shampoo and tepid water; a mohair wig can be cleaned with "Woolite" and cool water.

Dolls. Left: 13" H. Bisque head, composition baby body. Mark #D10. Right: 14" H. Bisque head, child's ball-jointed composition body. Collection of Lewis Longest Jr., FP, CPP.

Doll, 16" H. Kidalene body with bisque lower arms, dark blue fixed eyes, open mouth, four teeth. Mark #D10. Damaske collection.

Bisque figural dolls (no moving parts): Little Red Riding Hood 4" H. Indian maiden with a frog at her foot, 4" H. Dorland/Pegg collection.

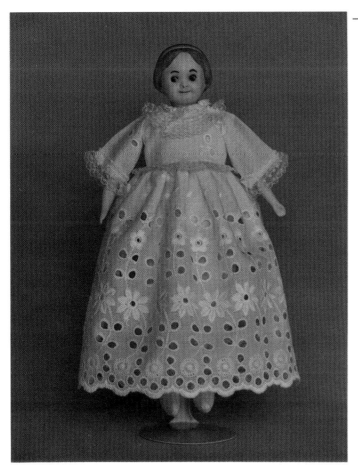

Doll, 10¾" H. Bisque socket head with painted orange hair and blue eyes, cloth body and legs with bisque lower arms. Mark #D8. Damaske collection.

Doll, 16" H. Bisque socket head, bent-limb composition body, blue sleep eyes, tongue, two teeth. Mark #D11.

Doll, 14" H. Bisque socket head on papier mache toddler body, light blue sleep eyes, open mouth, four teeth. Mark #D11. Damaske collection.

Dolls. Left: 13" H. China head with shoulder plate. Mark #D8. Right: 8" H. Bisque head and shoulder plate, forearms, and legs with original cloth body. Collection of Harold and Audrey Eklund.

Doll, 18" H. Bisque socket head, bent-limb composition body. Brown sleep eyes. Mark #D11.

Doll. 5½" H. Front row left to right: Molded bottle in hand, dome head, jointed arms and legs. Doll 8" H. Bisque head with shoulder plate, forearms, legs, original cloth body. Doll, 4½" H. Bisque with movable arms and legs, painted on shoes and bow in hair. Mark #D8. Doll, 7" H. Bisque dome head, five-piece composition body, painted eyes. Mark #D8. Back row left to right: Doll, 14" H. Bisque socket head, composition body, blue eyes Mark #D11. Doll, ll" H. Bisque head with brown sleep eyes, open mouth with two teeth, original wig, bent-limb composition body. Mark #D10. Doll, 12" H. Dome head boy, brown sleep eyes, bent-limb composition body. Mark #D11. Collection of Harold and Audrey Eklund.

Doll. 14" H. Bisque socket head on bent-limb composition body, dark grey fixed eyes, open mouth with two teeth. Mark #D10. Damaske collection.

Doll boy, 21" H. Bisque socket head on an excellent large German (K&R) bent-limb "oyster shell" composition body, brown fixed eyes, open mouth with two teeth. Mark #D4. Damaske collection.

Doll 11½" H. Bisque socket head on a bent-limb composition body, blue sleep eyes, open mouth with tongue and four teeth. Mark #D11. Damaske collection.

Doll boy, 19" H. Bisque socket head, bent-limb composition body, brown sleep eyes, mohair wig, tongue, two teeth.

Doll boy, 11½" H. Solid dome socket head with painted hair on bent-limb composition body, brown sleep eyes, open mouth with two teeth. Mark #D11. Damaske collection.

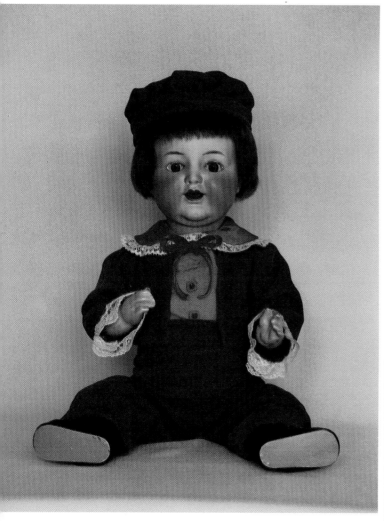

Doll boy, 20" H. Bisque socket head on bent-limb composition body, fixed light blue eyes, open mouth with tongue and two teeth. Mark #D11. Damaske collection.

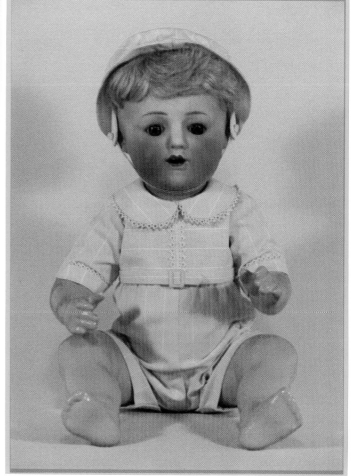

Doll boy, 16½" H. Bisque socket head on bent-limb composition body, blue sleep eyes, open mouth with two teeth. Mark #D11. Damaske collection.

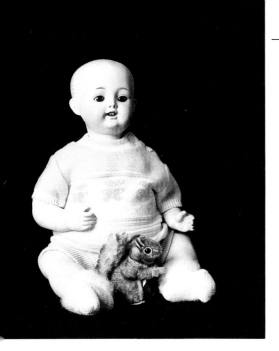

Doll boy 18" H. Solid dome head with painted hair on bent-limb composition body, brown sleep eyes, open mouth with two teeth mark #D3.

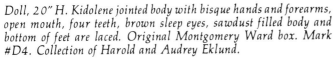

Doll, 20" H. Kidolene jointed body with bisque hands and forearms, open mouth, four teeth, brown sleep eyes, sawdust filled body and bottom of feet are laced. Original Montgomery Ward box. Mark #D4. Collection of Harold and Audrey Eklund.

Doll boy 14" H. Closed mouth "Pouty" character baby, bisque socket head on bent-limb composition body, brown sleep eyes, and original reddish-blonde mohair wig. Mark #D10. Damaske collection. Rare.

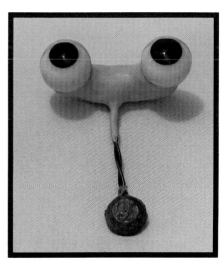

Glass weighted eyes which have the FY Nippon mark. The majority of eyes found in Nippon dolls are not marked in any way and it is very unusual to find a pair that are marked Nippon. Damaske collection.

Child's tea set, chickens with flowers in their mouths. Collection of Lewis Longest Jr., FP, CPP.

Three Oriental dolls in original boxes, 5" H. Box reads in typical Japanese fashion up and down:
A baby from the orient
I bring you greetings true
My smile brings luck
My hues will cheer
May fortune be with you. Mark 28. Collection of Harold and Audrey Eklund.

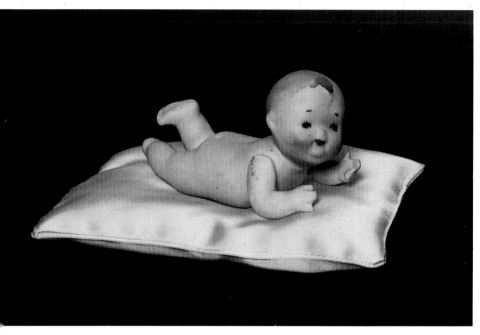

Doll, 4½" H. Original red crepe paper dress and hat. Figural doll, 3" H. holding loaf of bread and broom. Mark #D8. Collection of Wayne and Barbara Bryant.

Doll piano baby, 2⅛" H. X 4" W. Collection of Lewis Longest Jr., FP, CPP

Child's feeding dish, 7" W. Collection of Lewis Longest Jr., FP, CPP.

Miniature blown-out child's face, salt and pepper on tray. Tray 2" W. X 3⅝" I. Shakers 1⅝" H. Rising sun mark. Harold and Audery Eklund collection.

Figural bisque dolls (no moving parts) Red Cross nurse, 4" H. Figural Swiss Miss, 2⅛" H. Mark #D8. Collection of Harold and Audrey Eklund.

Doll Glossary

ALL-BISQUE BABIES: Usually range in size from 4" to 7" high. Most have character faces or stances and are jointed at the shoulders only; some have joints at the hips, and a very few have swivel heads. They can have molded-on or painted-on clothes, shoes and hair.

BALL-JOINTED: Usually a body of composition with wooden balls at the knees, elbows, hips, shoulders and sometimes wrists to make swivel joints.

BENT-LIMB BABY BODY: Composition body of five pieces with chubby torso and curved arms and legs.

BISQUE: Unglazed porcelain, usually flesh tinted, used for doll's heads or all-bisque dolls.

CHARACTER DOLL: Dolls with bisque or composition heads, modeled to look lifelike, such as infants, young or older children, young ladies, and so on.

COMPOSITION BODY: Generally made of such items as wood pulp, glue, sawdust, or various other sundry substances.

INTAGLIO EYES: Painted eyes with a sunken pupil and iris.

KID BODY: Doll body made of kidskin (skin of young goats) stuffed with material. The stuffing may be rag, cotton, shredded cork, etc. Kid bodies were made in two duplicate pieces sewn together along the edges. The stuffing was usually worked in as the sewing progressed.

KIDALINE BODY: Imitation bodies made to look like kid but with a linen or oil cloth texture. They were advertised by Morimura Brothers from 1919 to 1921. In 1922 Langfelder, Homma & Hayward imported these imitation kid bodies from Germany.

MOHAIR: Fine glossy hair of the Angora or Thibetan goat widely used in making doll wigs.

SHOULDER HEAD: Head and shoulders all in one piece.

SLEEP EYES: Eyes which are open when the doll is upright, but closed (turning to show eyelids) when the doll is laid down. This automatic action is controlled by a small weight. The eyes of sleep-eye dolls are normally made of glass or glass and ceramic and are generally lifelike in appearance.

SOCKET HEAD: Head and neck which fit into an opening in the shoulder plate or the body.

SOLID DOME HEAD: Head with no crown opening; could have painted hair or be covered by a wig.

TODDLER BODY: Usually a chubby ball-jointed composition body with chunky, shorter thighs and a diagonal hip joint; sometimes has curved instead of jointed arms; or occasionally made of five pieces with straight chubby legs.

Mark D1
Only this one mark and set of numbers has been recorded.

Mark D2
This particular mark has the name NIPPON spelled in a V-shape under the RE diamond but no numbers have been recorded with it so far.

Mark D3
This particular mark with the name NIPPON spelled straight under the RE diamond can be found with or without numbers usually located on top or off-center of the top of the diamond. Various numbers found with this particular mark are:

| Nos. 04 | Nos. B8 |
| A9 | B9 |

Mark D4
This mark has the words MADE IN NIPPON spelled in a V-shape under the RE diamond. It can be found with or without numbers that are usually located on top or off-center of the top of the diamond. Various recorded letters and numbers found with this mark are:

Nos. a10	Nos. B9
A4	B1001
A5	

Mark D5
This similar mark has the initials BE in the center of the diamond and the name NIPPON spelled in a V-shape underneath it. Numbers again are found at the top or off-center of the top of the diamond. Numbers recorded with this mark are:
Nos. 4
05

Mark D6
Only this one mark and set of numbers has been recorded.

Mark D7
The name NIPPON and numbers are located below the initial. Various numbers found with this mark:
No. 70018 (403)
No. 70018 (406)

NIPPON

Mark D8
Can be found with just the incised name NIPPON or have numbers or initials located on top or under or after the name such as the following:

Nos. 0	Nos. 102
3	105
5	123
84	144
97	221
98	A3
99	D
101	E

Mark D9
Various number and the word NIPPON are located beneath this initial are:
No. 03601 (600)
No. 76012 (601)
No. 76018 (30/3)

Mark D10

(Seperated FY)
Can be found with just the initials and the name NIPPON below or most likely will have 3 digit numbers beneath the name NIPPON. Various numbers found with this separated FY initial include:

Nos. 301	Nos. 406
303	464
401	505
402	601
404	602
405	

Mark D11
(Scrolled FY)
Numbers are located below the scrolled initials and above or above and below the word NIPPON. Various sets of numbers found with this particular scrolled FY include:

NO. 17604 (604)	NO. 76018 (406)
NO. 70018 (004)	NO. 76018 (603)
NO. 70018 (406)	NO. 76018 (604)
NO. 76018	NO. 76018 (2001)
NO. 76018 (30/6)	
NO. 76018 (Z0/1)	
NO. 76018 (403)	

Mark D12
According to our records, only these numbers have been found with this particular scrolled FY and both sets appear above the name NIPPON.

Mark D13
Only two different numbers have been recorded so far with this mark and they are located in the top part of the circle. They are:
NO 1
B9

Mark D14
Only this one mark and set of numbers has been recorded.

Mark D15
RE Nippon

Mark D20
ATA, Imperial Nippon

Mark D26
Chubby, L.W & Co., Nippon

BABY BUD
NIPPON

Mark D16
Baby Bud, Nippon, incised

Mark D17
Manikin, Nippon sticker

Mark D21
Nippon M incised,
#12 denotes size
doll; M is for
Moumura Bros.

Mark D22
MB (Mourmira Bros)
Baby Darling sticker
found on dolls.

Mark D27
Kid Doll, M.W. & Co., Nippon

Mark D18
Baby Doll, m.W. & Co. Nippon, sticker

Mark D23
Queue San Baby sticker

Mark D24
Dolly sticker on dolls,
sold by Morimura Bros.

Mark D28
Jollikid sticker (red and white)

Mark D29
Ladylike sticker (red and gold

NIPPON

Mark D30
Nippon incised.

Mark D19
SNB, Nippon

Mark D25
Sonny sticker (gold, red, white & blue)

Chapter Twentyfour
Plaques

The difference between a plate and a plaque is that a plaque has two holes drilled on the inside of the ridge on the back of the object. These holes were used to run a piece of wire or thread through in order to facilitate wall hanging. Plates have no holes. The difference between a plaque and a charger is the width, a plaque is 6"W to 12"W. A charger is 13"W or over. A cake plate always has two open pierced handles.

Birds in Nippon land.

Mountain and water wheel scene with swans. Plaque. 10¼" H. Maple leaf mark. Private collection.

Plaque swans molded-in-relief band 11¼" W. M-in-wreath mark. Private collection.

Egrets and Kingfisher on a branch 10" W. M-in-wreath mark. Private collection.

All 10" W. M-in-wreath mark.

Plaque "Venetian Gondola" 10" W. M. In wreath and a Private collection. "Neptune Warship" 9.5" W. Wreding collection. 10" W. In wreath and a Private collection.

Japanese sailing ship and scene. 9.75" W. M. In portable and in a collection of Bobbie and Vincent Droste.

Plaque 10" W. M. In wreath and in a home owner collection.

Plate. 10" W. Darlach collection. Plaque 10" W. M. In wreath and in a collection.

Plate 192

Dogs in Mettlach ware.

Dogs is the best loved of all animals, figure prominently in legend and
fiction, in art and on the symbolic of fidelity. In many cases the dog
is placed at the feet of women to symbolize affection and fidelity.

St. Bernard, Plate III W. M. F. wreath mark. Collection of
Bettie and Virginia Hensley.

Plaque 10" W. Moriage trim.

Top Plaque 8" W. Moriage trim border. Plaque 10" W. Maple leaf mark. Collection of Jess Berry and Gary Graves.

Hunting dogs, pointers. 10" W. M-in-wreath mark. Private collection.

Plaque 9" W.

Bull dog, plaque 12" W. M-in-wreath mark. Dorland/Pegg collection.

Plaques from left to right. 10¼" W. M-in-wreath mark. 1. Champion Monarch. Monarch won his title in England in 1878. 2. Center plaque and left whiskey jug. Champion L'Ambassodeur- owned by a Mr. C.G. Haptons, was the first American bred Champion in 1896. 3. Right plaque and right whiskey jug. Champion Rodney Stone-a Sheffield English Bulldog owned by Walter Jefferis whose dogs were world renown. Rodney held both English and American titles and was sold to an American for the then unheard of sum of $5,000.

Bulldogs are said to be one of the oldest breed of dogs known to man. Accounts of very early days in the history of England state that ancient Britons took large, ferocious and formidable dogs in battle against the enemy. It is believed that the Bulldog evolved from an intermixture of the English Mastiff and the war dogs of long ago.

The Bulldog received his name from his main function, which was to attack the bull. Earlier than the 17th century and well into the early 1800s, it was believed that the meat of a bull would not be worth eating unless the bull was baited by a dog. Thus the Bulldog was bred for its tenacious courage and vicious nature.

When bull baiting was outlawed (around 1820), dog fighting became one of the principal forms of sport in England. This left the purebred Bulldog of that day to be cross-bread with Terriers, producing a breed known as the Pit Bull. The Pit Bull was not only vicious, but fast and agile, making him eminently suitable to the sport. Dog fighting was responsible for the rapid move toward extinction of the purebred Bulldog.

This barbaric sport was outlawed in England in 1860, leaving fanciers of Bulldogs to gentle and refine the breed, and to set standards by which the purebred dog could be recognized. Dog shows gained in popularity as did the interest in breeding the perfect English Bulldog. In 1875, Bulldog breeders banned together forming the Bulldog Club Inc. Today it is the oldest breed club in the world still in existence. In April 1890, H.D. Kendall called a meeting of all Bulldog fanciers at Mechanics Hall in Boston to form a club known today as The Bulldog Club of America. These clubs devoted to the refinement of the Bulldog breed both in England and America did much to foster both the interest and popularity of the purebred dog. With the advent of World War I, interest and breeding of Bulldogs declined.

The Champion Bulldogs commemorated on our strains of Champion dogs have been found featured on plaque's, humidors, ashtrays, large cigarette or cigar boxes and wine jugs. To date these Bulldogs have never been found on vases.

Plaque 10½" W. M-in-wreath mark. Dorland/Pegg collection.

"Dutchman and the cat." 10" W. M-in-wreath mark. Private collection.

"Waiting by the shore." 10" W. M-in-wreath mark. Private collection.

"Waiting by the dock." 10" W. Dorland/Pegg collection.

"Three dancing children." Animal border. 10" W. M-in-wreath mark. Private collection.

"Arabs at the wall." 10" W. M-in-wreath mark. Private collection.

"Children in the wheat." 10" W. Maple leaf mark. Private collection.

"Farmer plowing". 10" W. M-in-wreath mark. Dorland/Pegg collection.

"Hay wagon." 11" W. M-in-wreath mark. Private collection.

"Man in a boat" 11½" W. M-in-wreath mark. Dorland/Pegg collection.

Scenic Plaques

Plaque 11" W. M-in-wreath mark. Dorland/Pegg collection.

Winter scene plaque 10" W. M-in-wreath mark. Collection of Ted and Nita Ensign.

Winter scene, with enameled grapes and grape vines. 10" W. M-in-wreath mark.

Winter scene with deer. 8¾" W. M-in-wreath mark. Collection of Stanley Jones.

"Elk in the mountains" plaque 10½". Dorland/Pegg collection.

All 10" W. All M-in-wreath mark. Private collection.

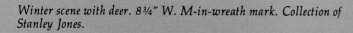

Charger 14¼" W. M-in-wreath mark. Collection of Lewis Longest
Jr., FP, CPP.

All 10" W. All M-in-wreath mark. Private collection.

*Charger 14¼" W. M-in-wreath mark. Collection of Lewis Longest
Jr., FP, CPP.*

Cake Plate 11¾" W. Scalloped edged, open pierced handles, heavy gold, with pink and white roses. Maple leaf mark.

Platter 13¼" W. Maple leaf mark.

Plaque 10⅞" W. Heavy gold with enameled jewels. Maple leaf mark.

Cake plate 11¼" W. Combination of scenic and floral, with enameled border. EE Nippon mark.

"Trailing Wisteria" plaque 10" W. Maple leaf mark.

Cake plate ll" W. Open pierced handles. Maple leaf mark.

Plaque 10" W. Collection of Lewis Longest Jr., FP, CPP.

Plate ll" W. Maple leaf mark. Collections of Jess Berry and Gary Graves.

Plaque 12" W. Maple leaf mark. Collections of Jess Berry and Gary Graves.

Plaques 10" W. Floral.

Chapter Twentyfive
Rectangular Plaques

Because rectangular plaques were hand molded rather than fitted inside a mold, the surface on some is slightly wavy rather than smooth. Their backs have four hanging holes rather than two (this was done so that the hanging wire could be placed on either side depending on which way the scene was painted on the plaque). They are all marked with the green M-in-wreath mark, and measure 10¼" W x 8¼" H. At the present time, only twelve rectangular plaques are known, making all of them scarce.

Four other known rectangular plaques are not pictured here.
"The Clipper Ships," "The Snowy Egrets," "Sail boats with enamelded grapes," and "Horse and Dog."

"Still life fruit." Rare. Collection of George and Doris Myers.

"Sheep grazing." Enameled border. Scarce. Collection of Ted and Nita Ensign.

"Egyptian Warships." Scarce.

"Arab by the campfire." Scarce.

"Indian Hunters" Scarce.

"Cows drinking in the stream."

"Polo player." Very Rare. Private collection.

"Saint Bernard." Scarce.

Chapter Twentysix
Game Sets

Game set Platter 13" x 18", six matching plates each 8¾" W. M-in-wreath mark. Rare. Collections of Jess Berry and Gary Graves.

Game set platter 12" x 17" six matching plates showing different birds 8¾" W. M-in-wreath mark. Rare. Collection of Jess berry, Gary Graves.

Fish set platter 9½" x 23" five matching 8½"W plates. Sauce dish with under plate M-in-wreath mark. Scarce. Collection of Jess berry, Gary Graves.

Chapter Twentyseven
Vases

12" H. M-in-wreath mark. Excellent high quality art work. Dorland/Pegg collection.

8" H. Private collection.

16" H. M-in-wreath mark. Ring
pretzel handles. Close up showing
excellent art work. Private collection.

6½" H. M-in-wreath mark.
Private collection.

8" H. M-in-wreath mark. Collections of Jess Berry and Gary Graves.

11¼" H. M-in-wreath mark. Ribbon handles, molded bottom. Pink enameled Trailing Wisteria and heavy gold overlay. Scarce. Collection of Rolfes and Virginia Hensley.

"Barn and chickens" 7¼" H. M-in-wreath mark. Collection of Cathy Keyes.

Pair 12" H. M-in-wreath mark. Showing front and reverse side of vase. Stand up handles. Collection of George and Donna Avezzano.

8" H. M-in-wreath mark. Sea Serpent handles. Collection of Rolfes and Virqinia Hensley.

10" H. M-in-wreath mark. Collection of Howard and Shirley Grubka.

9¾" H. Loop Handles. M-in-wreath mark. Collection of Rolfes and Virginia Hensley.

12" H. M-in-wreath mark. Collection of Rolfes and Virginia Hensley.

8" H. Snow scene with silver overlay.

14¼" H. Maple leaf mark. Heavy gold overlay designs and beading, four different scenic panels, each enhanced with gold border. Collection of Rolfes and Virginia Hensley.

13¾" H. M-in-wreath mark. Stand up handles. Collection of Rolfes and Virginia Hensley.

13¾" H. Maple leaf mark. Collections of Jess Berry and Gary Graves.

Basket 9" H. Maple leaf mark. Collection of Howard and Shirley Grubka.

9" H. EE Nippon mark.
Collection of Wayland and
Brenda Horton.

10" H. four footed. Royal Kaga
mark. Collection of Lewis Longest
Jr., FP, CPP.

14¼" H. M-in-
wreath mark. Three
ring pretzel molded
handles. Collection of
Rolfes and Virginia
Hensley.

8" H. Rare snow sceen with polar bears.

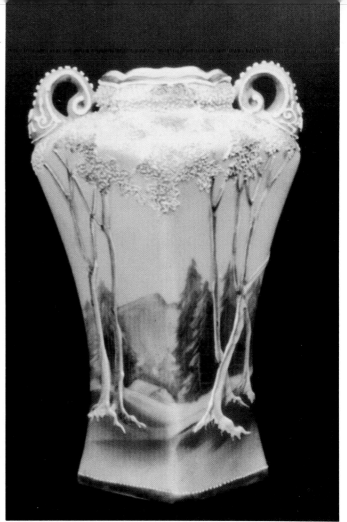

"White Woodland" 9" H. Maple leaf mark. Private collection.

"Cows grazing by the stream" 12½" H. M-in-wreath mark.

9½" H. Maple leaf mark. Ruffled top opening, free standing ring pretzel handles, heavy jeweling with eagles outlined in gold. Private collection.

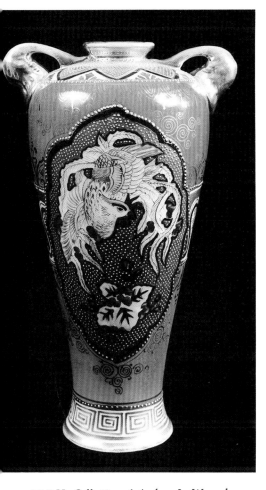

9¼" H. Collection of Andrea L. Waysok.

7¼"H. 9" H. 8" H. M-in-wreath mark. Pigtail handles. Collection of Bartley and Catherine Casteel.

13½" H. M-in-wreath mark. Private collection.

6" H. 4½" H. Collection of Bartley and Catherine Casteel.

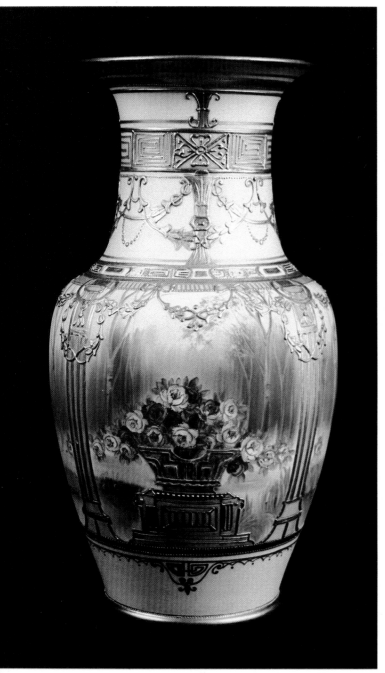

16½" H. M-in-wreath mark. Close up shows excellent quality of porcelain and art work. Note the heavy gold overlay designs. Collection of Rolfes and Virgina Hensley.

12" H. China EOH mark. Collection of Lewis Longest Jr., FP, CPP.

*ll" H. Maple leaf mark. Ribbon handles slightly molded-in-relief top
and bottom bands.*

15" H. Maple leaf mark. Collection of Phil and Jeanne Fernkes.

14½" H. Maple leaf mark. Three ring pretzel handles.

ll" H. Maple leaf mark. Collection of Rolfes and Virginia Hensley.

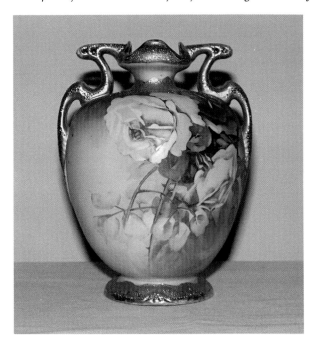

10¼" H. Plushy rose. M-in-wreath mark. Collections of Jess Berry and Gary Graves.

Pair 10" H. M-in-wreath mark. Collection of Lewis Longest Jr., FP, CPP.

12½" H. M-in-wreath mark. Three footed and three handled. Collection of Andrea L. Waysok.

7½" H. M-in-wreath mark. Ruffled top opening, ring pretzel handles. Collection of Rolfes and Virginia Hensley.

11¾" H. Maple leaf mark. Ruffled top opening, ring pretzel handles. Collection of Rolfes and Virginia Hensley.

8½" H. Collection of William and Irma Lusson.

8½" H. Maple leaf mark. Four footed. Private collection.

9¾" H. Maple leaf mark. Ruffled top opening, Ring pretzel handles.

7" H. Maple leaf mark. Collection of Rolfes and Virginia Hensley.

12" H. M-in-wreath mark. Scissor handles. Collection of Rolfes and Virginia Hensley.

12" H. Bolted Moriage urn. Royal Moriye mark. Private collection.

11½" H. M-in-wreath mark. Elephant handles. Collection of Andrea L. Waysok.

10" H. Maple leaf mark. Collection of Ralph and Cheryl DeWitt.

10¼" H. Collection of Ralph and Cheryl Dewitt.

11¼" H. Collection of Ted and Nita Ensign.

13" H. M-in-wreath mark. Ribbon handles. Collection of Olin and Grace Harkleroad.

14" H. M-in-wreath mark. Collection of Olin and Grace Harkleroad.

10" H. M-in-wreath mark. Trailing Wisteria. Collection of Ralph and Cherly DeWitt.

10¼" H. Red and gold with heavy jewels. Collection of Ted and Nita Ensign.

9¾" H. M-in-wreath mark. Collections of Jess Berry and Gary Graves.

12" H. Soft paste. Imperial Nippon mark. Collection of Lewis Longest Jr., FP, CPP.

12" H. Collection of Lewis Longest Jr., FP, CPP.

11" H. Cows grazing in the meadow. Collection of Lewis Longest Jr., FP, CPP.

9 1/4" H. Maple leaf mark. Collection of Wayne and Barbara Bryant.

Vase 6 1/2" H. Vase 8" H., Vase 8 1/2" H. M-in-wreath mark. Collection of Bartley and Catherine Casteel.

9" H. M-in-wreath mark. Collection of Cathy Keys.

Chapter Twentyeight
Woodland

Pedestal based tea set, pot, cream, sugar, six cups and saucers. Maple leaf mark. Collection of Rolfes and Virginia Hensley.

Woodlaand scene Vase 8½" H. Maple leaf mark. Collection of Stanley Jones.

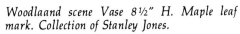

Dresser Set, Tray 12" W. Footed hair receiver, footed powder box, closed hat pin holder. Blue Maple leaf mark. Collection of Rolfes and Virginia Hensley.

Woodland vase 5½" H. Collection of Rolfes and Virginia Hensley.

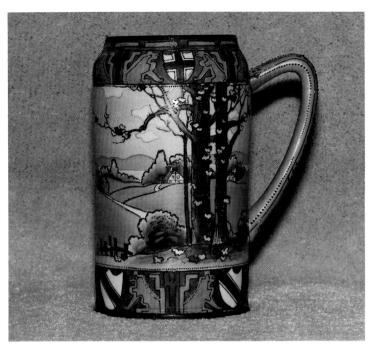

Stein 7" H. Collection of Roger Zeefe.

Woodland dish 8½" W. Maple leaf mark. Collection of Stanley Jones.

Vase 7" H. Maple leaf mark. Collection of Rolfes and Virginia Hensley.

Ring handled Nappy 8" W. Maple leaf mark. Collection of Stanley Jones.

Woodland scene Vase 10" H. Covered urn 8" H. Dorland/Pegg collection.

Man on a Camel

*Arab by the campfire. Vase 14"
H. M-in-wreath mark. Collection
of Rolfes and Virginia Hensley.*

*Arab by the campfire. Wine jug
9¾" H. M-in-wreath mark.
Collection of Rolfes and Virginia
Hensley.*

*Arab at Oasis. Vase 9½" H.
M-in-wreath mark. Collection
of Lewis Longest Jr., FP, CPP.*

*Arab By The campfire. Plaque 10" W. Rectangular plaque 11" H.
x 8" W. Green M-in-wreath mark.*

Arab at Oasis. Vase 11" H. Maple leaf mark. Collection of Ralph & Cheryl De Witt.

Arab at Oasis. Vase 10" H. M-in-wreath mark. Collection of Bartley and Catherine Casteel.

Man on a camel. Moriage trees. Scissor handles. Vase 9½" H. M-in-wreath mark. Collection of Lewis Longest Jr., FP, CPP.

Arab by the campfire. Vase 12" H. M-in-wreath mark. Dorland/Pegg collection.

Man on a camel. Stand up handles. Vase 6½" H. Maple leaf mark. Collection of Jan Eldridge.

Man on a camel vase 12¼" H. Moriage trees. Greek Key handles. M-in-wreath mark. Dorland/Pegg collection.

Man on a camel. Chocolate Set. M-in-wreath mark. Collection of Ralph and Cheryl DeWitt.

Man on a camel. Bowl 6" H. x 6" W. Collection of Cathy Keys.

Man on a camel. Vase 9½". Blue Maple leaf mark. Collection of George and Doris Myers.

Man on a camel. Vase 8¾". Elephant handles. M-in-wreath mark. Collection of Lewis Longest Jr., FP, CPP.

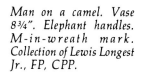

Chapter Thirty
Unusual

Cobalt and floral shaving brush. Unmarked. Collection of John and Francile McLain.

Heart shaped covered box 5½" x 4¾".

Butterfly shaped covered box.

Turtle shaped flower arranger with five holes. Blossom hand painted mark. Collection of Harold and Audrey Eklund.

Piano shaped covered box. Maple leaf mark.

Bisque figurine. Incised Nippon. Dorland/Pegg collection.

Porcelain figurine. Incised Nippon. From the collection of Wesley Wilson.

Bronze elephant frame. Incised Nippon, Porcelain insert. Collection of Ted and Nita Ensign.

Dogs of Foo are found at the entrance of temples to guard against evil. Purportedly they came into Japan from Korea along with the teachings of Buddha.

Cloisonné on porcelain vase 8" H. This Cloisonné on porcelain resembles the other cloisonné items except that it was produced on a porcelain body rather than a metal body. The decoration is divided into cells called cloisons. These cloisons are divided by strips of metal wire which kept the colors separated during the firing. Collection of Harold and Audrey Eklund.

Figural bird 4¼" H. Ballerina figural doll 3¼" H. Figural bisque match holder 3" H. Figural owl napkin ring 4" H. Dorland/Pegg collection.

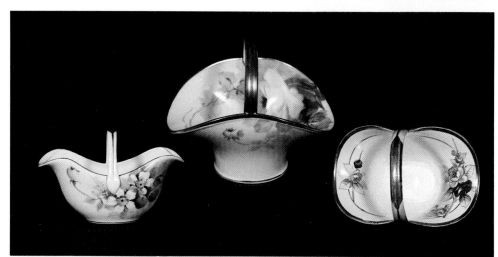

Three baskets left 3½" H. x 5¼" W. Rising sun mark. Center 5¼" H. x 6½" W. M-in-wreath mark. Right 4½" H. x 5¼" W. Private collection.

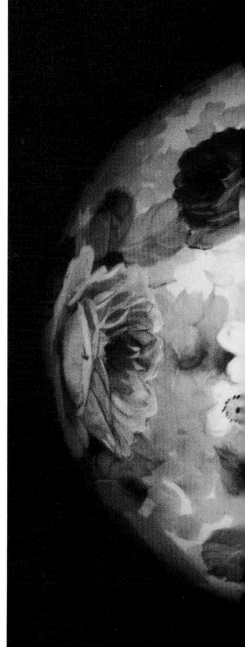

Figural Nipper and horn dish, right and left. Center figural dashound dish. 6" W. Dorland/Pegg collection.

Copper luster, possibly decorated by Pickard. M-in-wreath mark.

Dresden type figurines. Dorland/Pegg collection.

Novelty molded dish. Rising sun mark. Collection of Harold and Audrey Eklund.

Speak no evil, see no evil, hear no evil monkeys in two sizes. 2¼" H. and 2" H. Collection of Bob and Flora Wilson.

Hanging lamp shade. Very Rare. Dorland/Pegg collection.

Chapter Thirtyone
Miscellaneous

Ewer, 9" H. Maple leaf mark. Private collection.

Tankard, 11½" H., Maple leaf mark. Collection of Lewis Longest Jr., FP, CPP.

Pitcher, 4¼" H. M-in-wreath mark. Collection of Dr. and Mrs. Jody Ginsberg.

Pitcher, 9" H. Howard and Shirley Grubka collection.

Pitcher, 10" H. Howard and Shirley Grubka collection.

Beverege set. Pitcher, 8¼" H., Cups 5¼" H. M-in-wreath mark.

Ewer, 9" H. M-in-wreath mark. Howard and Shirley Grubka collection.

Cookie Jar, 7¼" H. Collection of William and Irma Lusson.

Cracker Jar. Collection of William and Irma Lusson.

A Cookie Jar 7¼" H. Water wheel scene. M-in-wreath mark.

Moose ferner, 4¼" H. x 5¾" W. M-in-wreath mark. Collection of Dr. and Mrs. Jody Ginsberg.

Moose basket, 5" W. M-in-wreath mark. Collection of Wayne and Barbara Bryant.

Ferner, 7" W. X 3" H. M-in-wreath mark. Collection of Bartley and Catherine Casteel.

Lion ferner, M-in-wreath mark. Scarce. Polly Frye collection.

Ferner. Phil and Jeanne Ferneks collection.

Although at first glance these two items look alike, there is one very distinct difference. One is a pancake server with a small air hole in the lid for the steam to escape. The other "Man in a Boat scene" is a covered butter dish without a hole in the lid.

*Lion cake plate, 10" W. M-in-wreath mark. Scarce. Collection of
Harold and Audrey Eklund.*

*Ferner with original tin liner, 10" W. x 6½" H. Pitcher, 5" H.
Maple leaf mark. Private collection.*

Bowl, 6¼" W. M-in-wreath mark. Collection of Dr. and Mrs. Jody Ginsberg.

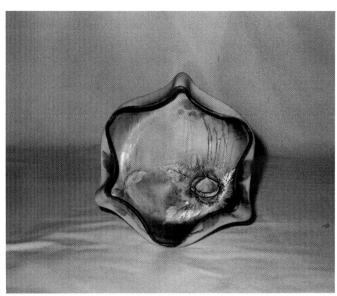

Bowl, 7½" W. M-in-wreath mark. Collection of Ted and Nita Ensign.

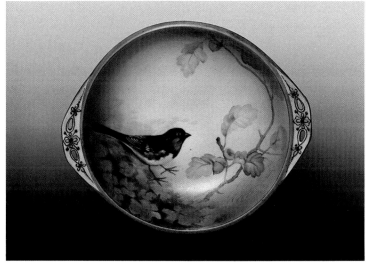

Bowl, 7" W. M-in-wreath mark. Collection of Lewis Longest Jr., FP, CPP.

Bowl 11¼" H. Maple leaf mark. Collection of George and Doris Myers.

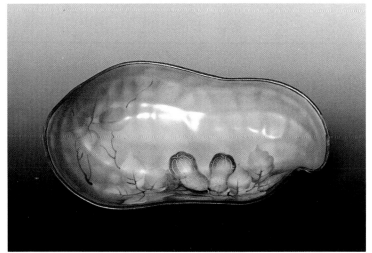

Bowl, 8" W. x 4¼" H. M-in-wreath mark. Collection of Lewis Longest Jr., FP, CPP.

Bowl, 7½" W. M-in-wreath mark. Collection of Ted and Nita Ensign.

Cream pitcher and sugar bowl sets. Howard and Shirley Grubka collection.

Cream pitcher and sugar bowl. Creamer, 3" H. Sugar, 3" H. Crown mark. Collection of Bartley and Catherine Casteel.

Cream pitcher and sugar bowl set. Creamer, 3¾" H., Sugar, 4½" H. M-in-wreath mark. Collection of Bartley and Catherine Casteel.

Banquet punch bowl. M-in-wreath mark. Olin and Grace Harkleroad collection.

Cream pitcher and sugar bowl set. Collection of William and Irma Lusson.

Creamer pitcher, 3" H. Sugar bowl, 4" H. M-in-wreath mark.

Potpourri jar. A complete potpourri jar consists of three pieces: the jar, a solid inner lid, and a top lid with holes. The jar was filled with rose petals which give out a sweet aroma when the inner, solid lid is removed and the pierced cover is used. During storage, the solid lid is inserted once again to confine the aroma inside the jar. 4½" H. M-in-wreath mark. Collection of Wayne and Barbara Bryant.

Loving cups, 6" H. X 5½" H. Collection of Wayne and Barbara Bryant.

Jam jar. Howard and Shirley Grubka collection.

Sugar shaker, 6½" H. Howard and Shirley Grubka collection.

Covered jar, 5¼" H. Maple leaf mark. Collection of Dr. and Mrs. Jody Ginsberg.

Potpourri jar, 5" H. Collection of Bartley and Catherine Casteel.

Cruet, 5" H. Maple leaf mark. Hanging match holder, 4½" H. Advertising "White Rock" match holder. Collection of Bartley and Catherine Casteel.

Tooth pick holders. Collection of William and Irma Lusson.

Shaving mugs, all 3¾" H. From left to right: M-in-wreath mark,
Maple leaf mark, Rising Sun mark, Rising Sun mark. Collection of
Lewis Longest Jr., FP, CPP.

Mustache cup with scalloped edge saucer. Maple leaf mark.
Collection of Wayne and Barbara Bryant.

Tea tile, 6½" W. M-in-wreath mark. Napkin ring, 2¼"
W. M-in-wreath mark. Collection of Bartley and Catherine
Casteel.

*Gravy boat with underplate. M-in-wreath mark. Lewis Longest Jr.,
FP, CPP.*

*Some Nippon items were designed to be a liner for polished copper or
nickel plate holders made by the "Manning Bowman Co." which
specialized in manufacturing and designing pots, pans, ladles and
funnels. Each of these holders is individually style numbered and
engraved "Manning Bowman quality, Meriden, Connecticut."*

*The Manning Bowman company was founded in Middletown,
Connecticut in 1832. In 1872, they moved to Meriden, Connecticut
where they remained until 1946. The Nippon-marked porcelain
inserts are referred to in the Manning Bowman catalogs as "Hand
Decorated Imported China Linings."*

Condiment set. Tray, 6" W. Tooth pick, 1 3/4" H. Mustard, 2 3/4" H. Salt and pepper, 2 1/2" H. M-in-wreath mark. Collection of Bartley and Catherine Casteel.

Spoon holder, 7 1/2" W. x 2 1/2" H. Butter tub with pierced insert, ice was placed in the bottom of the tub. M-in-wreath mark. Collection of Bartley and Catherine Casteel.

Salt and pepper shakers, 3 1/2" H. M-in-wreath mark. Harold and Audrey Eklund.

*Footed trinket box, 3¾" W. Maple leaf mark. Stamp box, 2¾" W.
M-in-wreath mark. Child's chamberstick, M-in-wreath mark.*

*Dutch shoes, all 3" W. M-in-wreath mark. Bob and Flora Wilson
collection.*

Triangular napkin ring holders, unmarked.

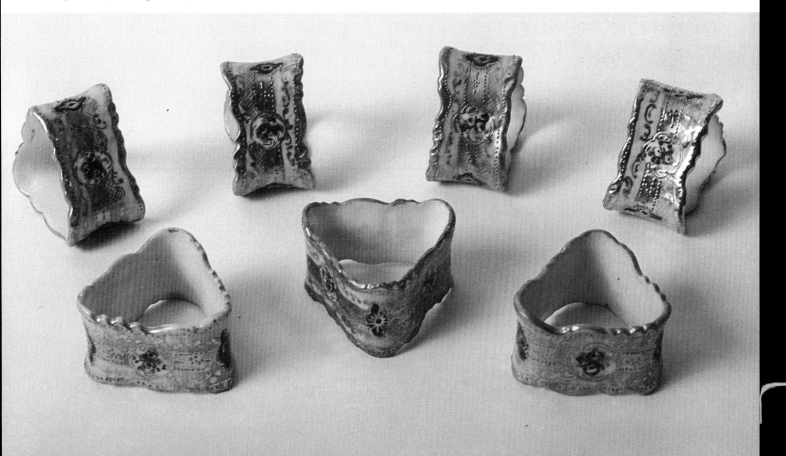

Chapter Thirtytwo
Souvenirs

Bowl 8" W. Magenta M-in-wreath mark. Collection of Bartley and Catherine Casteel.

Souvenir items showing a decal portraying a turn of the century Capital Building in Washington, D.C. Left to right: Creamer, 2½" H. M-in-wreath mark. Nappy, 7½" W. RC hand-painted Nippon mark. Footed trinket box, 2½" H. RC mark. Toothpick holder, 2¼" H. M-in-wreath mark. Lewis Longest Jr., FP, CPP.

Souvenir tray, 12¼" W. "Mount Rainier and Lake Washington." SNB blossom Nippon mark. Collections of Jess Berry and Gary Graves.

Chapter Thirtythree
Reproductions

"Antique Rose" pattern mug 4⅞" H., Green Maple leaf mark.

"Orchid" pattern, small pitcher 3½" H., Green Maple leaf mark.

There are many Nippon reproduction items on the market today. However, most of these current reproductions do not even slightly resemble Nippon era wares. Yet many collectors and dealers are fooled by the counterfeit backstamps on these fakes.

As stated in Title 18 of the United States Code of Federal Regulations, Section 2320, the term counterfeit means "(1) a spurious mark that is used in connection with trafficking in goods or services; (2) that is identical with or substantially indistinguishable from a mark registered for those goods or services on the principal register in the United States Patent and Trademark Office and in use, whether or not the defendant knew such mark was so registered; (3) the use of which is likely to cause confusion, to cause mistake or to deceive." Title 18 also states that it is illegal to traffic counterfeit goods or services into the United States.

Another law that buyers and sellers of antiques and collectibles should be aware of is Title 19 of the United States Code of Federal Regulations, Section 1304. It states that "every article of foreign origin imported into the United States shall be marked in a conspicuous place as legibly, indeliby, and permanently as the nature of the article will permit in such manner as to indicate to an ultimate purchaser in the United States the English name of the country of origin of the article." In other words, it is illegal to import or sell an item with a counterfeit mark. It its also illegal to remove any tags or marks that designate the country or origin on a piece.

Counterfeit Nippon items are manufactured today in Japan and Taiwan with one of three bogus Nippon marks found under the glaze. In addition, a paper sticker declaring the country of origin ("Made in Taiwan" or "Made in Japan") is applied to the items so that they will clear customs. Antique dealers can buy these wares in wholesale amounts from importing firms and then remove the paper stickers. In this manner, fake Nippon items showing only the counterfeit Nippon backstamp are made ready for the antique market.

The United States Customs agents actively seek help in identifying and prosecuting anyone who imports reproductions and counterfeits or anyone who deliberatly removes country-of-origin tags. Contact the nearest United States Customs Office.

The three Nippon marks repeatedly reporduced are variations of the M-in-wreath, maple leaf and rising sun.

The distored M-in-wreath mark on the elk plaque is not that frequent. An authentic M-in-wreath mark has an M in the center of a wreath which is open at the top.

"Green Mist" pattern, sugar bowl with lid 4½" H. x 5½" W. Cup
2½" H., blue rising sun mark.

Pattern unidentified. Plate 3½" H.

"Texas Rose" pattern, ewer 8¼" H. x 7" W., Blue Rising Sun
mark.

"Wild Flower" footed box 4½" H. x 5" W., green M-in-wreath mark.

Elk landscape, Distorted green M-in-wreath mark.

Opposite page: *Pattern unidentified. Pitcher 6¾" H., Blue Rising Sun mark.*

The three Nippon marks repeatedly reproduced are
variations of the M-in-wreath, maple leaf and rising sun.

An authentic M-in-wreath mark has a M in the center
of a wreath which is open at the top. The counterfeit
mark has a hour glass in the center of a wreath which is
open at the bottom.

The counterfeit mark

The distorted M-in-wreath mark found on the elk
plaque is less frequently found.

In the authentic, the maple leaf mark is quite small,
while the counterfeit mark is exaggerated in size.

In the authentic rising sun mark, the extending rays
are open. The counterfeit rising sun mark show
connected rays extending from the sun.

All of these pattern can be found on a variety of items
such as chocolate sets, cream pitchers, sugar bowls, salt
and pepper sets, covered boxes, tea sets, night sets,
Ewers, tankards, bells, mugs, baskets, ink wells, perfume
bottles, candlesticks, covered cheese dish, tooth brush
holders, and tea strainers.

Marks

Mark #1

Maple leaf mark. Backstamp was issued in 1891 by the Morimura Brothers company and continued by the Noritake Company, which was founded in 1904. The Maple leaf mark was registered in Japan in 1911 and can be found in blue, green, and magenta. "Blue Maple leaf" mark was applied to differentiate blanks which were produced by subcontract factories against those of Morimura and Noritake's own factory produced blanks at a time when Morimura and Noritake did not really have factories of their own. This mark can be found on the majority of portrait and tapestry items. The Noritake company speculates that the Maple leaf mark was used until about 1911-1915.

Mark #2

Tree Crest and Maple leaf mark, hand-painted Nippon. Circa 1908.

Mark #3

Mount Fujiyama, Nippon, Circa 1900. Blue.

Mark #4

Noritake made in Japan mark.

Backstamp for items exported to the United Kingdom, this mark was registered in London in 1908.

Mark #5

Mark #6

Mark #7

Mark #8

Mark #9

Marks #5, 6, 7, 8, 9

These backstamps were issued in 1906 with Japanese and United States registry on 5/30/1911. Stamp was issued for wares for U.S. export. Can be found in green and blue. The R.C. stands Royal Ceramic or Royal Crockery. Royal Ceramic stands for fine china, and the majority of items bearing these marks are of very high quality white porcelain. Mark #6 comes in a combination of both red and green. The RC is in green the letters in red. Mark #7 can be found in both green and blue.

Royal Sometuke
NIPPON

ROYAL SOMETUKE
Nippon
SICILY

Marks #10, #11

These two marks were issued in 1906 for both domestic and foreign markets.

Hand Painted
NIPPON

Mark #14

Circa 1912, blue.

HandPainted
NIPPON

Mark #12

Issued 1906 to 1908, in a faint blue. This mark is sometimes known as "Komaru," It is also known as the "tree crest" mark, which was the clan crest or "mon" of the Morimura family, signifying "strength" (A tree, to be strong, depends on equal balance or support both above and below.)

Hand Painted
NIPPON

Mark #15

Beginning year of manufacture was 1906 for United States export, registration date is unknown.

NO. 16034
HandPainted
NIPPON

Mark #13

Issued in 1912. Komaru symbol, hand-painted Nippon. The Number 1604 indicates the pattern number.

NORITAKE
NIPPON

Mark #16

Manufacture began 1906 for United States Export, registration date unknown. Can be found in blue, green, magenta.

Mark #17, #18, #19

These marks were registered in 1906 for both the domestic market in Japan and for exportation to the United States. Mark #17 Royal Satsuma Nippon. The House of Satsuma crest, cross within a ring. Mark #18, Royal Kinran Nippon gold and blue. Mark #19 Royal Kinran crown Nippon found in blue, green and gold.

Mark #20

Royal Nishiki world Nippon. Items bearing this mark are generally produced on a soft paste or pottery body. Dark olive green color.

Mark #21

Manufacture began in 1906 for U.S. market. Japanese registry, 1911 in a shade of blue-black. China with this stamp also was sold undecorated to other factories and decorating studios at home and abroad. (See Studio decorated marks.)

Mark #22

M-in-wreath mark both United States and Japanese registry in 1911. The wreath was designed from the crest of the Morimuras: The "M" is also taken from Morimuras. This mark is found on the majority of Molded-In-Relief and Wedgewood items. Can be found in green, blue, and magenta with the most commonly found being green. The majority of items bearing the magenta M-in-wreath mark are utilitarian in nature. The Noritake Company speculates that they started phasing out the Nippon M-in-wreath mark beginning in 1918 and could have been used until 1921. Approximately 50% of Nippon found today has this mark.

Mark #23

This items were produced for the D.M. Read Company, Bridgeport, Conn. in honor of Fair Week 1912.

Mark #24

Noritake M-in-wreath mark was produced between 1912 and 1922 and is found in green.

Mark #26

Issued in 1912. The printing is done in red and the wreath in green.

Mark #27

Compliments of the Morimura Bros. Paper label found on Nippon items, 1913. Label is gold with black writing.

Mark #28

Rising Nippon. Circa 1916. This is not usually attributed to the Noritake Company, although it does appear on at least two Noritake patterns which were later named Azalea and Monterey. Possibly the Noritake Company purchased these patterns or took over the original pottery. Blue. The Rising sun mark is usually found on children's dishes, play tea sets and utilitarian items.

Mark #25

Produced and registered in 1914. This backstamp was used on the first dinner ware set to be produced by Noritake. "Sedan" is the pattern name. This same mark can be found with various names in place of "Sedan" and indicates pattern name.

Mark #29

OAC Hand-painted Nippon. Okura Art China was first issued in 1919 in the suburbs of Tokyo by Magobei Okura and his son, Kazuchika, who were also founders of the Noritake Company. Okura china is made of highly refined material and is fired at exceptionally intense heat for extreme strength and durability. It is fine-grained, smooth and rich with exquisitely hand-decorated designs painted by native artisans. Because of its supreme beauty and quality, Okura china has long been commissioned by the Japanese Imperial families and by Japanese Embassies throughout the world.

Mark #30, #31

Kinjo fish Nippon. Green, blue and magenta.

Mark #32

Pagoda hand-painted Nippon. This mark appears as a decal sticker under the glaze. This mark usually shows up on items of poor quality porcelain and art work. Blue.

Mark #33

Hand-painted IC Nippon.

MADE IN
NIPPON

Mark #34

Made in Nippon.

NIPPON

Mark #35

Nippon found as a backstamp on porcelain, incised on small bisque dolls, and other non porcelain Nippon items.

Mark #36

Shinzo Nippon, found in blue and magenta.

Mark #37

Made in Nippon tea cup.

Mark #38

Tanega hand-painted Nippon, found in magenta.

Mark #39

Yamato Nippon found in magenta.

Mark #40

The Yamato hand-painted Nippon.

Mark #41

Mythical Bird Ho, T Nippon. Turquoise.

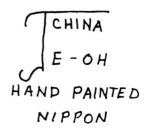

Mark #42

China E-O-H Hand-painted Nippon found in green, blue, and magenta. Objects with this backstamp are usually items of low quality porcelain and have poor artwork.

Mark #43

Hand-painted S & K Nippon, found in blue, green, and magenta.

Mark #44

Hand-painted S & K Nippon, found in blue, green and magenta.

Mark #45

Hand-painted TS Nippon.

Mark #46

Hand-painted T.S. Nippon, found in blue.

Mark #47

Double T Diamond, Nippon.

Mark #48

Hand-painted TN-wreath mark Nippon, found in red and green.

Mark #49

Hand-painted T Nippon.

Mark #50

Hand-painted C.G.N. Nippon, found in green.

Mark #51

JPL hand-painted Nippon.

Mark #52

NMC Nippon hand-painted.

Mark #53

Hand-painted Elite B Nippon.

Mark #54

Hand-painted E E Nippon.

BARA
HAND PAINTED
C O
V L
NIPPON

Mark #55

Bara Hand-Painted COL Nippon.

Mark #56

Hand-painted C.O.N. Nippon.

Mark #57

Sendɑi Hand-painted Nippon.

NIPPON

Mark #58

C O L Nippon.

Mark #59

Hand-Painted Coronation Ware Nippon.

Mark #60

Mark #61

HAND PAINTED

NIPPON

Mark #62

Hand Painted
NIPPON

Mark #63

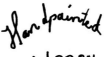

NIPPON

Mark #64

Mark #60, #61, #62, #63, #64

Hand-Painted Nippon.

NIPP ON
D

Mark #65

Nippon D

NIPPON
3

Mark #66

Nippon 3

A3
NIPPON

Mark #67

A3 Nippon

NIPPON 84

Mark #68

Nippon 84

NIPPON 144

Mark #69

Nippon 144

144
NIPPON

Mark #70

144 Nippon

221
NIPPON

Mark #71

221 Nippon

PATENT
NO 30441
NIPPON

Mark #72

Patent No. 30441, Nippon

ROYAL

NIPPON

Mark #73

Royal Dragon, Nippon

Mark #74

Meiyo China, Y, Nippon

Circle Marks

Mark #75

Imperial Nippon hand painted. Green and blue.

Mark #76

Oriental china Nippon found in blue.

Mark #77

Stouffer hand-Painted Nippon.

Mark #78

Circle M Nippon F24.

Mark #79

H in circle Nippon.

Mark #80

G in circle, hand-painted Nippon.

Mark #81

S in circle Nippon.

Mark #82

T-in-wreath mark circle hand-painted Nippon found in blue.

Mark #83

Mark #84

Royal Hinode Nippon in circle found in blue.

Mark #85

Shofu Nagoya Nippon in circle found in green.

Mark #86

SNB Nagoya Nippon in circle found in green.

Mark #87

Hand-painted Nippon in circle.

Mark #88

Hand-painted Nippon with symbol circle.

Mark #89

Superior Nippon in circle found in magenta.

Mark #90

Circle and crown hand-painted Nippon found in blue and green.

Mark #91

Circle and crown. Made in Nippon, found in blue and green.

Mark #92

Circle and symbols hand-painted Nippon.

Mark #96

Crown hand-painted Nippon found in green with red colors or plain green.

Mark #93

Circle and cherry blossom hand-painted Nippon, found in blue.

Mark #97

Crown with J.M.D.S..

Mark #94

Hand-painted Nippon in circle with symbol.

Mark #98

Royal Moriye crown mark, found in blue and green colors.

Crown Marks

Mark #95

Dowsie Nippon crown.

Mark #99

Crown Maruta Royal Blue Nippon.

Flowers and Leaves

Mark #100

Paulownia flowers and leaves hand-painted Nippon. (Crest used by the Empress of Japan kiri no mon) found in a combination of red and green colors.

Mark #101

Paulownia flower and leaves hand-painted Nippon (Crest used by Empress of Japan kiri no mon.)

Mark #102

Cherry blossom Nippon.

Mark #103

Cherry blossom hand-painted Nippon, found in blue green and magenta colors.

Mark #104

Double cherry blossom mark Nippon, found in blue and magenta.

Mark #105

Nippon mark with leaves.

Mark #106

M. M. hand-painted Nippon with flowers.

Mark #107

Carpathia M Nippon with leaves.

Mark #108

Chikusa hand-painted Nippon with flower and leaves.

Mark #112

Hand-painted Nippon with symbol.

Mark #109

Nippon with leaves, and symbol

Mark #113

Hand-painted Nippon with symbol.

Marks with Symbols

Mark #114

Royal Kuyu Nippon, blue plum blossom.

Mark #110

Royal Kaga Nippon.

Mark #111

Hand-painted Nippon with symbol.

Mark #115

Symbol M Nippon 10.

Mark #116

Hand-painted Nippon with symbol.

Mark #117

Hand-painted Nippon with symbol.

Mark #118

Nippon with symbol

Marks #120, #121, #122, #123, #124, #125

Nippon with Japanese symbol.

Mark #119

Nippon with symbol found in black.

Marks #126, #127

Torii Nippon found in turquoise, blue.

Mark #128

Nippon with symbol.

Mark #129

Patent Applied for 1911 made in Japan, mark found on Coralene in blue and magenta.

Mark #131

Nippon with symbol

Mark #132

Nippon with symbol

Mark #130

R.S. Nippon mark found on Coralene objects.

Bibliography

Ayars, Walter. *Larkin China*. Summerdale, Pa: Echo Publishing, 1990.

Bearne, Mrs. *A Court Painter and His Circle, François Boucher.* London: Adelphi Terrance, 1913.

Benet, William Rose. *The Readers Encyclopedia.* New York: Thomas Y. Crowell Company, 1948.

Clarke, Joseph I.C. *Japan at First Hand.* 1918

Coleman, Dorothy S., Elizabeth A., and Evelyn J. *The Collector's Encyclopedia of Dolls.* New York: Crown Publishers, 1968.

Coleman, Dorothy S., Elizabeth A., and Evelyn J. *The Collector's Encyclopedia of Dolls, Volume Two.* New York: Crown Publishers Inc., 1986.

Demarest's Monthly magazine, November, 1879.

Donahue, Lou Ann. *Noritake Collectibles.* Iowa: Wallace-Homestead Book Co., 1970.

Fermigier, Adre. *Millet.* Geneva: A. Skira Genva, 1977.

Funk & Wagnalls New Encyclopedia. Funk & Wagnalls, Inc.

Gaston, Mary Frank. *The Collectors Encyclopedia of R.S. Prussia.* Paducah: Collector Books, 1981.

Gillis, Rita. "Nippon Animal Kingdom." 1986.
    "Nippon Indians." 1991. New York: International Nippon Collectors Club Newsletter.

Kovel, Ralph and Terry. *Kovels' New Dictionary of Marks.* New York: Crown Publishers Inc., 1986.

Lucas, E.V. *Chardin and Vigée-Leburn.* London: Methuen & Co. Ltd., n.d.

Miller, Robert C. *Wallace-Homestead Price Guide to Dolls.* Des Moines, Iowa: Wallace-Homestead, 1975.

Muehasam, Gerd, ed. *French Painters and Painting From the Fourteenth Century to Post Impressionism.* New York: Frederich Ungar Publishing Company, 1970.

Pegg, Wilff and Jan Dorland. *The Nippon Chronicle.* Toronto, Canada:Infinity Graphics Limited, 1982, 1983.

Schroeder, Joseph, ed. *Sears Roebuck & Co. Catalogue.* Reprint 1971. Northfield, Illinois: DBI Books, Inc.

Schiffer, Nancy. *Japanese Porcelain 1800-1950.* Pennsylvania: Schiffer Publishing Ltd., 1986.

Schmidt, Minna M. *400 Outstanding Women Of the World and the Costumology of their time.* Chicago: Minna M. Schmidt, 1933.

Stitt, Irene. *Japanese Ceramics of the Last 100 Years.* New York: Crown Publishers Ltd, 1974.

Stryienski, Casimir, ed. *Memoirs of the Countess Potocka.* New York: Doubleday & McClure Company, 1901.

Swaim, Connie. "Customs Agents Seek Help in Tracking Fakes." Antique Week. Knightstown, Inc., 1990.

Van Patten, Joan. *The Collectors Encyclopedia of Nippon Porcelain, Series two.* Paducah: Collectors Books, 1982.

The Collectors Encyclopedia of Nippon Porcelain, series three. Paducah: Collectors Books, 1986.

World Book Encyclopedia. Field Enterprises Educational Corporation, 1966.

Wojciechowski, Kathy. *History of Hand Painted Nippon Porcelain.* Pennsylvania: Warman Publishing Company, 1985.

Updated and Revised Nippon Spotter. 1987.

Cobalt Nippon. New York: International Nippon Collectors Club Newsletter, 1988.

"Counterfeit Nippon marks fool unsuspection buyers." *Antique Week.* Knightstown, Indiana, 1988.

"Moriage predominant on export wares during Nippon Era." *Antique Week.* Knightstown, Indiana, 1989.

"The Best of Nippon." *Collector Editions.* Volume 18, No. 4. New York, 1990.

"Nippon Era Moriage." *Antiques & Collecting Hobbies* Volume 95, No. 7. Chicago, Illinois: Lightner Publishing Company, 1990.

"Nippon Porcelains Soar in Popularity." *New York-Pennsylvania Collector.* New York, 1990.

"The Ladies on Nippon Portraits." *Collector Editions.* Volume 19. Number 5. New York, 1991.

"Nippon Era Coralene." *Price Guide to Oriental Antiques.* Pennsylvania: Wallace-Homestead, 1991.

"A New Look at Nippon." *Antique Showcase.* Ontario, Canada, 1992.

Index

Value Guide

The current values in this book should be used only as a guide. They are not intended to set prices, which vary from one section of the country to another. Auction prices as well as dealer prices vary greatly and are affected by condition as well as rarity and demand. Neither the Author nor the Publisher assumes responsibility for any losses that might be incurred as a result of consulting this guide. The prices stated are for items in very good to mint condition. Damaged items, which have for instance hair line cracks, crowsfeet, cracks, or chips, or items that have been repaired have a greatly reduced value. Never expect full value for a damaged item.

Key to position abbreviations: b=bottom, c=center, l=left, r=right, t=top

Page No.	Position	Description	US dollars
1	c	Cracker jar	275-375
2	t	Calling card	125-185
	b	Basket	125-165
6	l	Tapestry vase, 6 1/2"H.	450-550
	r	Plaque, 10"W.	300-375
12	l	Monk wine jug	750-950
13	r	Chocolate pot, 12 1/2"H.	300-375
14	bl	Bowl	75-135
	tr	Tankard, 14"H.	275-375
15	t	Dresser set	575-675
16	bl	Pair of vases, 7 1/4"H.	135-185 each
	r	Vase, 11 1/4"H.	225-275
17	r	Covered urn, 11"H.	275-375
18	b	Portrait vases, 12"H.	950-1300 each
20	t	Corn sets	275-475
	br	All	275-375
21		Indian plaques, 10"W.	650-950
22		Moose plaques, 10"W.	450-650
25	b	Tray	145-185
26	l	Wine jug	475-525
	tr	Compote	125-165
	br	Bowl	175-275
27	b	Vase	145-225
32	l	Covered urn, 15 1/2"H.	3500-4200
	tr	Pair vases, 12 "H.	750-950 each
	br	Vase, 14 1/2"H.	1000-1200
33	cl	Plate, 9 3/4"W.	650-850
33	bL	Urn, 13 1/4"H.	1300-1500
		Plate, 9 3/4"W.	650-850
	c	Covered urn, 10"H.	1300-1400
34	c	Covered urn, 16"H.	2800-3000
35	c	Ewer, 12 1/4"H.	1100-1200
36	tl	Plate, 10"W.	475-575
	cl	Vases, pair, 8"H.	525-625 each
	bl	Plate, 10"W.	475-575
		Vase, 11"H.	875-975
	tr	Vases, pair, 8"H.	525-625 each
	br	Ewer, 6 3/4"H.	350-450
37	cl	Plate, 10"W.	475-575
	bl	Cake plate	2500-3500
	r	Vase, 12"H.	825-925
38	t	Covered urn, 11"H.	1100-1200
		Covered urn,	750-850
	bl	Plate, 10"W.	550-650
	br	Plate, 10"W.	375-475
39	tl	Vase, 8 1/2"H.	525-625
	cl	Plate, 10"W.	550-650
	bl	Plate, 10"W.	550-650
	tr-br	Vase, 8 1/2"H.	450-650 each
40	tl	Vase, 5 1/4"H.	375-475
	cl	Covered urn, 10 1/2"H.	1200-1300
	tr	Vase, 10"H.	675-775
	br	Ewer, 10"H.	575-675
41	tl	Vase, 9 1/2"H.	625-725
	cl	Vase, 8"H.	525-625
	tr	Plate, 12 3/8"W.	525-625
	b	Tea set	1100-1200
42	tl	Footed vase, 7 1/2"H.	550-650
	bl	Vase, 7 3/4"H.	475-575
	tr	Vase, 5"H.	425-525
	cl	Vases, 8"H.	575-675 each
		Vase, 4"H.	375-475
	br	Vase, 10 1/2"H.	725-825
		Plaque, 10"W.	650-750
43	tl	Vase, 6"H.	475-575
	bl	Tankard	1300-1500
	tr	Vase, 6"H	750-925
	br	Vase, 5 1/2"H.	375-475
44	tl	Vase, 11"H.	825-925
	bl	Jugs	375-475 each
	tr	Covered urn	1200-1400
	br	Dish	250-350
45	rl	Covered box	275-375
	cl	Plate, 10 1/2"W.	475-575
	bl	Plate, 10 1/2"W.	475-575
	tr	Plaque, 12 1/2"W.	575-675
46	tl	Vase, 6"H.	375-475
	cl	Plate, 8 3/4"W.	425-500
	bl	Trinket box	225-275
	tr	Plate, 10"W.	550-650
	br	Plate, 10"W.	550-650
47	tl	Bolted urn, 12 1/4"H.	950-1100
	bl	Plaque, 9 3/4"W.	525-625
	tr	Hanging vase	550-650
	br	Plaque, 9 1/4"W.	650-750
48	t	Dresser set	1400-1800
	br	Hair receivers	150-245 each
		Trinket box	145-185
		Hat pin holder	275-375
49	tl	Tooth pick holder	135-195
	cl	Cream and Sugar	225-275
	bl	Trinket box	225-275
	tr	Trinket box	225-275
	cr	Plate, 6 1/2"W.	225-275
	br	Humidor	185-250
50	tl	Cardinal plaques	800-925 each
	tr	Cardinal humidor	1200-1500
51	tl	Mug	375-475
	cl	Stein	475-575
	bl	Stein	440-550
	tr	Stein	475-575
	br	Wine jug	750-950
52	cl	Covered urn, 12 1/2"H.	825-925
	tr	Bolted covered urn, 17"	1800-2000
	br	Bolted covered urn, 16"	1400-1500
53	tl	Bolted covered urn, 16"	1400-1600
	tr	Bolted covered urn, 13 1/2"	1100-1200
	b	Bolted covered urns, 181/2"	2800-3600 pair
54	c	Covered urn, 14"H.	650-850
55	c	Covered urn, 13 1/2"H.	750-950
56	tl	Covered urn, 13 3/4"H.	675-775
	bl	Bolted covered urn, 15 1/2"	1400-1600
	tr	Covered urn, 10 /4"H.	575-675
	br	Bolted urn, 16"H.	1100-1300
57	tl	Bolted urn, 14 1/2"H	675-775
	tr	Bolted urn, 15 1/2"H.	750-850
	b	Bolted urns, 16 3/4"H.	1200-1300 each
58	tl	Bolted urn, 11"H.	675-875
	tr	Bolted urn, 14 1/2"H.	675-775
	b	Urns 1 and 2	750-950
		#3	575-675
59	t	Candle sticks	275-325 pair
		Trivets	145-175
		Bowl	150-185
	bl	Humidors	425-475
		Ashtrays	135-185
	br	Vase, 11 3/4"H.	375-475
60	t	Bowl	175-225
		Plaque, 10"W.	375-475
		Vase, 9"H.	295-325
	bl	Plaque, 10"W.	374-475
		Vases	275-375
		Covered box	250-350
	br	Plaque, 10"W.	325-400
61	t	Tankard set	1200-1400
	bl	Plaque, 10"W.	325-400
	br	Wine jug	875-975
		Humidor	750-850
		Wine jug	750-850
62	tl	Ashtray	135-185
		Plaques, 8 3/4"W	275-375
	b	Plaques, 7 3/4"W.	375-475
63	tl	Vase, 12 1/2"H.	625-725

	bl	Plaque, 11"W.	475-575	80	tr	Vase, 5 3/4"H.	225-325
	tr	Plaque, 11"W.	375-475		bl	Vase, 7 1/4"H.	325-385
	br	Vase, 11 1/4"H.	375-475		c	Vase, 9"H.	425-475
64	tl	Plaque, 10"W.	250-350		bc	Vase, 4 1/2"H.	225-285
		Hat pin holder	145-185		tr	Ewer, 10 1/4"H.	325-385
		Vase, 9 1/2"H.	275-375		br	Vase, 10 1/4"H.	325-425
	cl	Vase, 15"H.	1200-1400	81	tl	Vase, 11 1/4"H.	325-425
	bl	Bolted urn	375-425		bl	Vase, 11 1/4"H.	425-525
		Plaque, 11"W.	325-425		tc	Covered urn	425-475
	tr	Candle stick, 8"H.	225-300		bc	Covered urn, 8"H.	425-475
	br	Vase, 6 1/2"H.	200-285		tr	Vase, 10"H.	350-450
65	tl	Plaque, 10"W.	275-325		br	Vase, 10"H.	350-450
	cl	Plate	225-325	82	t	Tankard set	1300-1500
		Dish	135-185		b	Ewer, 6 3/4"H.	225-285
	tr	Vase, 5 1/2"H.	125-175			Ewer, 11 1/2"H.	225-285
		Vase, 8 1/2"H.	245-345			Ewer, 12"H.	375-475
	cr	Vase, 5 1/2"H.	125-175	83	t	Vases	300-500 each
		Mug, 5 1/2"H.	175-225		c	Vase, Ferners	185-285 each
		Vase, 7 1/2"H.	165-200		b	Chocolate set	1100-1300
		Vase, 8"H.	200-245	84	t	Dresser set	525-625
	b	Punch Set	1300-1700		b	Demitasse set	425-525
66	t	Vase, 7"H.	400-475	85	t	Match holder	165-200
		Vase, 4 1/2"H.	185-225			Humidor	425-525
		Vase, 9"H.	400-475		bl	Cracker jar	325-425
		Vase, 5"H.	185-225		cr	Basket, 5"H.	185-285
	c	Charger, 12 1/4"H.	375-475		br	Ferner	400-475
		Salt and Pepper	65-110	86	t	Tea set	1100-1300
		Toothpick	110-145		b	Chocolate set	475-625
		Tankard	425-525	87	c	Vase, 12"H.	1100-1300
	b	Cream and Sugar	195-145	88	tl	Ferner	285-385
		Chocolate pot, 10"H.	325-395		cl	Covered urn	375-475
67	tl	Ewer, 4 1/2"H.	225-325		bl	Ewer, 3 1/2"H.	175-225
	b	Tea set	475-575		tr	Ewer, humidor	350-450 each
	tr	Nappy	75-135		br	Vase, 6 1/2"H.	350-425
		Plate, 7"W.	65-125	89	l	Vase, 12"H.	475-575
	Cr	Spooner	225-325		tr	Ewer, 9 1/4"H.	325-400
68	tl	Covered box	75-135		br	Vase, 12"H.	400-475
		Vase, 6"H.	145-185	90	tl	Ewer, 6 1/4"H.	275-325
		Vase, 2 3/4"H.	95-125		cl	Ewer, 15"H.	475-575
	cl	Cream and Sugar	175-225		tr	Tea pot, 6 1/2"H.	275-325
	bl	Vase, 9 1/2"H.	325-425		c	Tea pot, 6 1/2"H.	200-275
		Pitcher	265-325		br	Ewer, 10 1/4"H.	350-425
	tr	Covered urn, 10"H.	325-425	91	c	Vase	1100-1300
	br	Basket vases, 8 3/4"H	125-275 each	92	t	Vases	275-475 each
69	tl	Bowl, 11"W.	225-275	93	tl	Vase, 7"H.	525-625
	bl	Cigarette box	225-275		b	Vase, 9 1/4"H.	575-675
	tr	Vase	225-325			Vase, 6 1/2"H.	375-475
	br	Vase, 7 1/4"H.	200-285		tr	Vase, 8"H.	375-475
		Vase, 15"H.	250-350	94	t	Vases	325-425 each
		Cracker jar	275-375		bl	Vase, 10"H.	525-600
70	tl	Stein	525-625		br	Vase, 9"H.	550-650
	cl	Humidor, 7"H.	750-850	95	tl	Vase, 11 1/4"H.	375-475
	tr	Loving Cup, 7"H.	325-425		bl	Vase, 8 1/2"H.	325-425
	cr	Vase, 9 1/2"H.	375-475		tc	Vase, 9"H.	400-475
71	r	Tankard, 13 1/2"H.	425-525		bc	Vase, 11"H.	450-550
72	l	Covered urn	340-475		tr	Hat pin holder	275-375
	c	Bolted covered urn, 18 1/2"	1800-2200		br	Vase, 10"H.	375-475
	r	Wine decanter, 14 1/2"H	475-575	96	tl	Chamberstick	285-325
73	tl	Humidor	475-575		cl	Basket	185-235
	bl	Vase, 8"H.	325-425		bl	Vases, 9 3/4"H.	275-375 each
	tr	Ewer, 7 1/2"H	325-425		tr	Vase, 7 1/4"H.	325-400
	br	Vase, 13 1/2"H.	350-450		br	Ewer, 10 1/2"H.	675-775
74	t	Cream and Sugar	175-275	97	tr	Vase, 12"H.	675-775
		Vase, 9 1/4"H.	375-475		b	Vase, 9 3/4"H.	450-550
	bl	Vase, 12 1/2"H.	475-575			Tankard 13 1/4"H.	750-850
	br	Vase, 8 3/4"H.	225-325			Ewer, 10 1/2"H.	1100-1200
75	l	Tankard, 13 1/2"H.	375-475		tr	Vase, 15"H.	725-825
	tr	Vase, 10 1/2"H.	325-425	98	tl	Covered urn 14"H.	1800-2000
	br	Vase, 9"H.	325-425		cl	Vase, 7 3/4"H.	425-525
76	tl	Charger, 13 1/4"W.	375-475		tr	Vases	175-375 each
	cl	Vase, 6 1/2"H.	275-375		cr	Basket	185-235
	bc	Ewer, 6"H.	275-375			Ewer	250-325
	r	Tankard, 14"H.	425-525			Vase, 3 1/4"H.	185-235
77	tl	Vase, 10 1/2"H.	375-475		br	Vase, 9"H.	375-475
	br	Vase, 7 1/2"H.	275-375	99	cl	Ferner	525-625
	tc	Vases	250-350 each		bl	Mug	175-275
	bc	Vase, 6 1/2"H.	275-375		tr	Candlestick, 8"H.	450-550
	cr	Basket, 8 3/4"H.	375-475		br	Vase, 6"H.	450-550
78	tl	Vase	525-625	100	tl	Cream and Sugar	225-325
	bl	Vase, 9"H.	375-475		cl	Candlesticks	350-450
	tr	Vase	375-475		tr	Vase, 9"H.	375-475
	br	Vase, 8 1/2"H.	375-475		cr	Vase	225-275
79	tl	Vase, 8 1/2"H.	400-450		bc	Vase, 9"H.	375-475
	bl	Vase, 9 1/2"H.	375-475		br	Basket	325-425
	tc	Vases	325-375	101	t	Rose bowl	650-750
	br	Vase, 9 1/2"H.	350-450		b	Bowl	525-625

102	c	Vase, 9"H.	850-950
103	c	Vase, 7"H.	750-850
104	tl	Vase, 8 1/4"H.	1100-1300 each
	cl	Vase, 8 1/4"H.	275-325
	b	Tea set	1000-1200
	tr	Vase, 11"H.	550-650
		Vase, 11"H.	650-750
105	r	Vase, 8 1/4"H.	975-1100
106	l	Ewer, 10 3/4"H.	900-1100
	tr	Vase, 8 1/4"H.	600-700
	br	Vases	675-875 each
107	tl	Vase, 8 1/4"H.	450-550
	bl	Vase, 7 1/4"H.	450-550
	tr	Vase, 8 1/4"H.	425-525
	br	Vase, 8 1/2"H.	425-525
108	t	Vase, 7"H.	425-525
	b	Vase, 7"H.	400-475
109	bl	Bolted urns	1300-1500 each
	r	Bolted urn	2800-3000
110	tl	Chocolate pot, 12 1/2"H.	450-550
	bl	Pitcher, 9 1/2"H.	750-850
	tr	Tea set	750-850
	br	Bolted urn	1600-1800
111	tl	Vase, 7 1/4"H.	425-525
	cl	Covered urn, 13 3/4"H.	1200-1400
	tr	Plates	300-475 each
	cr	Vase, 10 1/4"H.	750-850
	br	Dish	200-265
112	tl	Vase, 14"H.	650-750
	b	Vases, 9 1/4"H.	425-525 each
		Plaque, 10"W.	375-475
113	t	Cake plate	325-425
	b	Vase, 15 3/4"H.	575-675
		Vase, 12 1/2"H.	500-600
	r	Covered urn	425-525
114	t	Planter	125-185
	c	Basket, 6"H.	185-200
	b	Chocolate set	650-750
115		Candlelamps	1600-2000 each
116	l	Night lights	1500-1800 each
	r	Lamp	525-625
117	tl	Boudoir lamp	2200-2600
	tr	Portrait lamp	750-950
	b	Portrait lamps	3500-4500
118		Lamps	225-375 each

The scale from scarce to very very rare in regards to the Molded-In-Relief items is based on number of items known to exist, and is as follows:
Scarce-15-20
Rare- 10-15
Very Rare-5-10
Very Very Rare-2-5
Unique- 1 only

119	l	Rectangular plaque	4500-5500
	r	Humidor	1600-2200
120	tl	Vase, 8 1/2"H	2000-2500
	bl	Tankard set	5500-6500
	tr	Wine jug	2300-3200
	br	Humidor	1600-2200
	t	Rectangular plaque	1800-2500
	bl	Vase, 10"H.	1800-2000
	br	Plaque	1600-2000
122	tl	Vase, 12 1/2"H	2800-3000
	bl	Humidor	2300-2800
	tr	Plaque	1200-1500
	br	Vase, 10 1/2"H.	1300-1600
123	tl	Plaque, 12"W.	1300-1600
	b	Humidor	2200-2800
	tr	Vase, 9 1/2"H.	1000-1300
		Humidor	950-1100
124	t	Indian plaques	800-1100
		Wedgewood plaque	1300-1700
	br	Ashtray	600-675
125	tr	Humidor	2200-2800
	cl	Humidor	1200-1400
	br	Charger, 15"W.	1400-1900
		Plaque	400-500
126	tl	Ashtray	350-450
	cl	Plaque, 10"W.	2500-3000
	tr	Bookends	850-950

	br	Plaque	500-600
127	tl	Plaque, 10"W.	650-750
	cl	Humidor	650-750
	tr	Humidor	650-750
	bc	Plaque, 10"W.	900-1200
	br	Humidors	650-750 each
128	tl	Beggar man vase	1400-1800
	b	Camel humidors	1200-1700 each
	tr	Humidor	700-750
	cr	Plaque, 10 1/2"W.	725-825
129	t	Tankard set	2500-3500
	c	Plaques, 10 1/2"W.	1100-1300
	b	Plaque, 10 1/2"W.	450-550
		Humidor	600-700
130	tl	Ferner, Humidor	550-650 each
	cl	Tiger ashtray	650-750
	tr	Tiger humidor	1200-1300
	b	Vase, 6 1/2"H.	550-700
		Vase, 10 1/2"H.	750-850
		Vase, 7 1/2"H.	550-700
		Vase, tapestry	650-750
131	tl	Stein, 7"H.	650-750
	cl	Plaque, 10 1/2"W.	1600-1800
	b	Ashtray	500-550
	tr	Humidor	850-1300
	cr	Humidor	550-650
132	t	Charger, 15 1/2"W.	1400-1900
		Plaque, 10 1/2"W.	550-650
	cl	Ashtray	650-750
	bl	Ashtray	400-450
	r	Bulldog plaque	850-1100
		Wedgewood plaque	1300-1700
133	t	Eagle plaques	1100-1500
	cl	Eagle plaque	1100-1500
	bl	Eagle humidor	1400-1600
	cr	Eagle plaque	1300-1600
134	tl	Humidor	1000-1200
	bl	Stein, 7"H.	1000-1200
	tr	Vase, 10"H.	1500-1800
	br	Vase, 9"H.	1500-1800
135	tl	Ferner	450-550
	cl	Ashtray	950-1100
	bl	Ashtray	750-800
	tr	Humidor	825-1100
	br	Vase, 8"H.	1100-1300
136	tl	Bowl	525-725
	b	Humidor	1100-1300
	tr	Bowl	525-725
137	tl	Vase, 8"H.	850-950
	bl	Ferner	750-850
	tr	Humidor	850-11000
	br	Ferner	850-950
138	tl	Plaque	1000-1300
	bl	Vase, 10 1/4"H.	1200-1400
	cr	Vase, 5 1/2"H.	650-850
139	r	Bolted urn	2600-3200
	tr	Plaque, 10"W.	375-475
	cr	Plaque, 11"W.	375-475
140	tl	Stein	550-650
	bl	Plaque, 10"W.	250-350
	r	Humidor	850-950
141	t	Indian plaque, 10"W.	1200-1500
	bl	Ashtray	160-185
	br	Nappy	160-185
142	t	Cigarette box	250-350
	b	Humidor	1400-1500
143		Steins	350-550 each
144		Steins	350-550 each
145		Steins	350-550 each
146		Mugs	175-275 each
147		Mugs	175-275 each
		Stein	550-650
148		Jugs	975-1100 each
149	cl	Jug	275-375
	bl	Jug	475-575
	tc	Jug	625-725
	bc	Jug	475-575
	tr	Jug	625-725
	cr	Jug	475-550
150		Humidors	550-650 each
151	tl	Humidor	625-725
	cl	Humidor	375-475
	bl	Humidor	575-675
	tr	Humidor	550-650
	br	Humidor	400-475

152	tl	Humidor	650-750
	bl	Humidor	375-475
	tr	Humidor	425-525
	cr	Humidor	350-450
	br	Humidor	350-450
153	tl	Humidor	450-550
	b	Humidor	350-450
	tr	Humidor	350-450
	br	Ashtray	165-185
154	t	Humidors	225-325 each
	c	Cigarette boxes	200-275 each
	b	Ashtray	125-175
		Nappy	125-175
155	tl	Ashtray	125-225
	cl	Loving cup	75-135
		Match box holder	125-195
	bl	Ashtray	65-95
	tc	Ashtray, Match holder	125-225
	cr	Ashtray, Match holder	135-185
	br	Smoke set	850-950
156	tl	Desk set	1200-1400
	b	Desk set	350-450
	tr	Inkwell	175-225
		Rocking blotter	175-225
157	l	Chocolate set	325-425
	r	Chocolate pot	325-425
158	t	Chocolate set	650-750
	b	Chocolate set	225-285
159	t	Chocolate set	375-475
	c	Chocolate set	550-650
	b	Chocolate set	650-850
160	c	Chocolate pot	325-425
161	t	Chocolate set	950-1300
	b	Chocolate set	950-1300
162	t	Chocolate set	650-850
	b	Chocolate set	550-650
163	t	Chocolate set	750-850
	b	Chocolate set	265-365
164	t	Chocolate set	950-1300
	b	Chocolate set	1200-1500
165	t	Chocolate set	1200-1500
	c	Chocolate set	375-475
	b	Chocolate set	275-375
166	tl	Tea pot	120-165
	c	Tea set	325-385
	b	Tea set	375-475
	tr	Tea set	325-385
167	t	Demitasse set	850-1000
		Lemonade sets	135-185 each
168	l	Dresser set	475-575
		Perfume bottles	135-175 each
169	tl	Dresser set	300-400
	c	Perfume bottle	135-175
		Covered box	95-125
		Dutch shoe	185-225
	bl	Dresser set	300-400
	br	Perfume bottle	135-175
170	t	Lady's spitton	150-250
		Perfume bottle	135-175
		Ring tree	65-125
	bl	Hat pin holder	85-145
	br	Stick pin holder	145-200
171	tl	Hat pin holder	85-135
	c	Tooth brush holder	85-135
		Large powder boxes	250-350
	br	Hat pin holders	85-135
172	tl	Covered boxes	125-165
	c	Ring trees	65-125
		Basket	65-125
		Dutch Shoe	185-225
	br	Hair pin holders	95-135

NOTE: All doll prices are for dolls that are clean, undamaged and well-dressed. They MUST have good to excellent quality bisque with appropriate bodies that are in need of NO repair.

173		Doll, 23"H.	625-725
174	tl	Half doll	90-140
	cl	Doll, 2"H.	900-1000
	br	Doll, 21"H.	575-675
175	l	Doll, 21"H.	575-675
	c	Doll, 19"H.	450-550
	r	Doll, 21"H.	575-675
176	tl	Doll, 16"H.	275-375
	b	Figural dolls	125-185 each
	tr	Doll, 13"H.	200-300

		Doll, 14"H.	225-325
177	tl	Doll, 10 3/4"H.	75-125
	bl	Doll, 14"H.	225-325
	tr	Doll, 16"H.	275-375
	br	Doll, 13"H.	185-285
		Doll, 8"H.	100-150
178	t	Doll, 18"H.	350-450
	b	Back row doll	225-325
		Doll	175-275
		Doll	195-295
		Front row doll	100-150
		Doll	125-160
		Doll	85-135
		Doll	100-150
179	tl	Doll, 14"H.	225-325
	bl	Doll, 11 1/2"H.	175-275
	tr	Doll, 21"H.	700-800
	br	Doll, 19"H.	450-550
180	cl	Boy doll, 20"H.	525-625
	tr	Boy doll, 11 1/2"H.	175-275
	br	Boy doll, 16 1/2"H.	300-400
181	t	Boy doll, 18"H.	350-450
	c	Pouty doll, 14"H.	1000-1250
	b	Doll, 20"H.	575-675
182	t	Child's tea set	225-300
	b	Three dolls	180-230 each
183	tl	Piano baby	125-175
	bl	Salt and Pepper	95-145
	tr	Doll, 4 1/2"H.	95-145
		Figural doll	100-150
	cr	Feeding dish	75-125
184	t	Nurse	125-175
		Swiss Miss	75-125
187	tl	Plaque, 10"W.	250-350
	b	Plaques	225-300 each
	tr	Plaque	275-375
	cr	Plaques	275-375 each
188	tl	Plaques	225-275 each
	cl	Plaque	275-375
	be	Plaque	225-275
	tr	Plaques	250-350 each
	cr	Plaque	250-350
	br	Plaque	225-275
189	t	Plaque	350-450
	bl	Plaque	825-925
	br	Plaque	350-450
190	l	Plaque, 8"W.	275-375
		Plaque, 10"W.	350-450
	tr	Plaque	350-450
	br	Plaque	250-350
191	t	Plaque	1200-1400
	b	Plaque	825-925
192	t	Plaques	425-525 each
		Jugs	750-850 each
193	tl	Plaque	225-275
	cl	Plaque	250-350
	bl	Plaque	225-275
	tr	Plaque	250-350
	br	Plaque	275-375
194	tl	Plaque	350-450
	bl	Plaque	350-450
	tr	Plaques	250-350 each
	cr	Plaque	250-350
195	all	Plaques	325-425 each
196	r	Plaques	225-325 each
	l	Plaques	145-185 each
197	tl	Plaques	145-185 each
	cl	Plaque	145-185
	b	Plaque	350-450
	r	Plaques	225-300
198	tl	Cake plate	325-400
	bl	Plaque	185-225
	tr	Platter	225-300
	br	Cake plate	145-185
199	tl	Plaque	250-350
	bl	Plaque	145-185
	tr	Cake plate	185-225
	br	Plate	325-425
200	all	Plaques	185-225 each
201	tl	Rectangular plaque	1100-1200
	b	Rectangular plaque	850-950
202	tl	Rectangular plaque	750-850
	B	Rectangular plaque	1100-1200
	tr	Rectangular plaque	1100-1200
203	tl	Rectangular plaque	850-950
	b	Rectanqular plaque	1100-1200

	tr	Rectangular plaque	850-950
204	c	Game set	2200-2600
205	t	Game set	2200-2600
	b	Fish set	1900-2300
206	l	Vase, 12"H.	550-650
	r	Vase, 8"h.	275-375
207	l	Vase, 16"H.	975-1100
	r	Vase, 6 1/2"H.	225-275
208	tl	Vase, 8"H.	185-285
	b	Pair vases, 12"H.	550-650 each
	tr	Vase, 11 1/4"H	375-475
	cr	Vase, 7 1/4"H.	185-225
209	yl	Vase, 8"H.	275-375
	bl	Vase, 10"H.	375-425
	tr	Vase, 9 1/4"H.	200-250
	cr	Vase, 12"H.	375-475
	bc	Vase, 8"H.	275-375
210	l	Basket, 9"H.	375-475
	tr	Vase, 14"H.	550-650
	br	Vase, 13 3/4"H	400-500
211	tl	Vase, 9"H.	135-175
	cl	Vase	175-200
	bl	Vase, 14 1/4"H.	875-975
	r	Vase, 8"h.	275-375
212	l	Vase, 12 1/2"H.	550-650
	tr	Vase, 9"H.	400-475
	br	Vase, 9 1/2"H.	225-285
213	tl	Vase, 9 1/4"H.	145-185
	bl	Vase, 6"H	75-135
		Vase, 4 1/2"H.	55-75
		Vase, 7 1/4"H.	135-175
	tr	Vase, 9"H.	165-225
		Vase, 8"H.	125-165
	br	Vase, 1 1/2"H.	375-475
214	l	Vase, 16 1/2"H.	2300-2800
	b	Vase, 10"H.	350-450
215	c	Vase, 11"H.	375-475
216	c	Vase, 15"H	750-850
217	c	Vase, 14 1/2"H.	850-950
218	l	Vase, 12 1/2"H.	375-475
	tr	Vase, 11"H.	375-475
	cr	Vase, 10 1/4"H.	375-475
	br	Vases pair	275-300 each
219	tl	Vase, 11 3/4"H.	325-425
	bl	Vase, 8 1/2"H.	285-325
	tr	Vase, 7 1/2"H.	275-325
	cr	Vase, 8 1/2"H.	245-300
	br	Vase, 9 3/4"H.	275-325
220	tl	Vase, 7"H.	145-185
	bl	Vase	450-550
	tr	Vase, 12"	325-425
	br	Vase, 11 1/2"H.	325-425
221	tl	Vase, 10"H.	225-325
	cl	Vase, 10 1/4"H.	225-325
	bl	Vase, 14"H.	325-425
	tr	Vases	325-425 each
	br	Vase, 10"H.	225-300
222	tl	Vase, 9 1/4"H.	225-275
	bl	Vase, 12"H.	145-195
	tc	Vase, 10 1/2"H.	225-325
	cr	Vase, 12"H.	135-185
	br	Vases pair	325-400 each
223	tl	Vase, 9 "H.	225-275
	b	Vases	200-225 each
	tr	Vase, 9"H.	225-275
224	tl	Vase, 8 1/2"H.	275-325
	b	Dresser set	750-950
	tr	Tea set	900-1000
	cr	Vase, 5 1/2"H.	175-275
225	tl	Stein, 7"H.	625-725
	cl	Vase, 7"H.	275-325
	bl	Nappy	125-185
	tr	Dish	125-185
	br	Vase, 10"H	325-375
		Covered urn	550-650
226	tl	Vase, 14"H.	550-650
	b	Plaque, 10"W.	325-425
		Rectangular plaque	1100-1200
	tc	Wine jug	925-1200
	tr	Vase, 9 1/2"H.	300-375
227	tl	Vase, 10"H.	300-375
	Bl	Vase, 9 1/2"H.	450-550
	tr	Vase, 11"H.	300-375
	br	Vase, 12"H.	450-550
228	tl	Vase, 6 1/2"H.	185-250
	cl	Vase, 12 1/4"H.	550-650
	tr	Chocolate set	550-650

	c	Vase, 9 1/2"H.	185-250
	cr	Bowl	135-185
	br	Vase	185-250
229	tl	Covered box	275-326
	tr	Shaving brush	145-185
	b	Covered box	275-325
230	l	Piano	375-475
	tr	Flower arranger	175-275
	br	Bisque figurine	225-325
231	tl	Figurine	125-185
	bl	Foo dogs	1300-1500
	tr	Bronze plaque	145-185
	br	Cloisonne vase	450-550
232	tl	Basket, 3 1/2"H.	55-75
		Basket, 5 1/4"H.	110-135
		Basket, 4 1/2"H.	55-75
	cl	Figural Nipper	150-200 each
		Dashound dish	350-450
	bl	Copper luster	45-100 each
	bc	Hanging lamp shade	1300-1500
233	tl	Dresden type figurines	135-185 each
	tr	Novelty dish	95-135
	cr	Monkeys, 2 1/4"H.	185-245
		Monkeys, 2"H.	155-185
234	l	Tankard, 11 1/2"H.	275-325
	r	Ewer, 9"H.	325-375
235	tl	Pitcher, 9"H.	275-325
	c	Pitcher	275-325
	bl	Beverage set	275-325
	tr	Pitcher, 4 1/4"H.	145-185
	br	Ewer, 9"H.	275-325
236	tl	Cookie jar	225-325
	bl	Cookie jar	375-475
	tr	Cracker jar	145-185
	cr	Ferner	175-225
	br	Basket	75-125
237	tl	Ferner	125-185
	bl	Pancake server	225-275
	tr	Ferners	175-225 each
	br	Covered butter dish	275-375
238	t	Cake plate	325-375
	b	Ferner	225-275
		Pitcher, 5"H.	75-125
239		Bowls small	75-110 each
		Bowl, 11"	225-275
240		Cream and Sugars	125-175 each
241	tr	Cream and Sugar	125-175
	c	Cream and Sugar	125-175
	b	Cream and Sugar	185-235
242	t	Cream and Sugar	125-175
	c	Cream and Sugar	75-115
	b	Punch bowl	450-550
243		Cream and Sugars	75-125 each
		Potpourri jar	135-185
244	tl	Loving cups	65-135 each
	cl	Sugar shaker, 6 1/2"H.	175-275
	cr	Covered jar	135-185
	br	Potpourri jar	135-185
245	t	Cruet	115-155
		Match holder	125-185
		Match holder	75-125
	b	Tooth pick holders	75-135 each
		Tooth pick holders	65-95 each
		Tooth pick holders	55-95 each
246	t	Shaving mugs	85-195 each
	c	Mustache cup	135-185
	b	Tea tile	85-125
		Napkin ring	45-95
247	t	Gravy boat	185-225
	b	Manning Bowman	
		Sherbet	75-135 each
		Plate	115-145
		Set	135-185
248	t	Condiment set	95-145
	c	Spoon holder	85-110
		Butter tub	85-110
		Salt and Pepper	55-95
249		Trinket boxes	95-195
		Chamber stick	45-95
	c	Dutch shoes	185-225
	b	Napkin rings	65-135 each
250	c	Bowl	175-225
251	t	Creamer, 2 1/2"H.	40-80
		Nappy	85-145
		Trinket box	125-175
		Tooth pick holder	85-125
	b	Tray, 12 1/4"H.	250-300